Do Moore, Get More

THE ROAD TO YOU

Dan Moore

FRANKLIN
STREET
BOOKS

Do Moore, Get More / Dan Moore. —1st ed.

Author photo by Bridgette Marie Balmes
Book cover design by Jetlaunch.net

ISBN 978-1-64184-207-5 (pbk)
ISBN 978-1-64184-208-2 (eBook)

Contents

For Kelley and our girls,
Sydney, Samantha, and Sofia

When I discover who I am, I'll be free.

—Ralph Ellison

FOREWORD

There was an evening, almost two years before the writing of this book, when I knew my friend Dan Moore was on to something big.

We had been friends for years before this evening. During our talks, we would always discuss our plans, our goals, and how we both wanted to perform large-scale actions that helped others.

But this night in early 2018 was different. There was a certain energy—almost an audible "buzz"—that was constant in our conversation.

I had just made the decision to sign with a major talent agency in NYC, but I had no interest in discussing that. I was far more interested in hearing Dan talk about THE IDEA.

Dan had very recently—as in, earlier in the day—had an awakening. It was kind of an "Aha, I can't believe this is all connected" moment he had while on the flight from his then home in Sacramento to NYC. The kind of moment filled with thoughts so big that the desire or need to discuss them with someone you trust is so strong that you almost need to puke the idea out of your mind and check whether your thoughts are earth-shattering or thirty-five minutes away from having you committed to the mental wellness ward of your local hospital.

I was blessed to be the person of trust that evening.

Dan's idea, though a little more matured and framed slightly differently than what you are about to expose your mind and conscious to (and thank God for that, because the "framing" was the only bad part of the idea), was one that left me nearly speechless for the entire duration of that dinner.

It was the idea that nearly everything in one's life is either directly or indirectly related to everything else, and that self-awareness of this one fact would open the door to true happiness, self-worth, sense of purpose, and true satisfaction.

This idea, or truth, as I too have come to realize, is the combination to the hardest lock in life to open.

The fact that one's self-awareness can be so immensely powerful that it can literally change the course of his or her life from reactive, forced servitude and basic misery to controlled, purposeful, everlasting satisfaction is one that I literally cannot wait for you to realize, learn, and hone for yourself.

Of all the people I know, both personally and professionally (not to brag, but I know a powerful and influential person or two), there is nobody better alive today to present this truth to you than Dan Moore.

So, let me do what I do best, which is get out of the way, and page by page, let you get closer to the lessons, actions, and results Dan has for you in the pages to follow.

One piece of advice from me before you continue...

GET READY, because there is Moore here than the title implies.

Frank Lopes
Author of Success in Seven
President, Get More Frank Productions
VP, FBDigital Marketing & Advertising Agency

INTRODUCTION

Y ou aren't broken. You aren't lost. You haven't wasted your life. You aren't a bad person. You haven't missed your calling. You're just *stuck*! And you're stuck for one simple reason: you're not fully self-aware.

We're bombarded day-in and day-out by quotes and posts and videos about hustling and grinding and sleepless nights and insane exercise regimens, and they're all seemingly designed to lead us to believe that we're failing if we aren't shooting for the moon every minute of every day. But what if we aren't necessarily looking to reach the moon? What if we'd be perfectly content on some other planet (or just here on earth), feeling whole and purposeful and happy? Through social media and the internet in general, we have access to so many extraordinary people that, at times, it's easy to become overwhelmed while trying to figure out simply how to elevate our lives just a bit above the status quo. Before we know it, we've gotten ourselves on that path to the moon, and we're miserable—because the moon is not even close to the place we're meant to be.

What I really want to know (and, more importantly, what you really want to know) is, *who are you* (underneath all the layers of who you've come to *think* you are)? What is your unique path to happiness? What gives you joy? What makes you feel fulfilled? What are the boundaries within which you can fall asleep each night at peace with yourself and the life you've created?

As far as who I am, well, I'm just some guy—some guy who knows what it's like to have fears, wonder whether or not I'm enough, wish for a better life, deal with failure, and generally want more. I'm also a guy who believes, without a doubt, that you are capable of far more than you think you are.

I've had ups and downs and experienced a few unexpected losses over the course of my life. We all have. Mine included a failed long-term relationship, a significant loss of income, and—most impactful of all—a complete loss of self. These setbacks came at different times in my life, and I never saw any of them coming because I was neither aware of nor in any way paying attention to what was going on around me and within me. I wasn't ready to look in the mirror and shed the denial that was holding me back. The big question is, are you ready to do that? I assume that the answer is—to one degree or another—yes, because you're here. Throughout the following pages, I'll detail my own journey through the struggles of feeling "stuck" in specific moments—a journey that led to discovering and unlocking the radical influence and impact of self-awareness.

This book is about giving you back the power to transform your life by showing you how critical *authentic*, stripped-down, fully bared self-awareness is in that process.

Even as an avid reader, I've admittedly never been one to pick up books about self-awareness specifically. I was hyper-focused on motivation and success, and it never occurred to me that self-awareness was the precursor to either. It seems that I'm not the only one who has thought of self-awareness as something that just magically shows up or is obtained through osmosis once you reach a certain level in life. I got lucky and bumped my head on it earlier than many do, although I didn't see it fully blossom until I was in my forties. I'm hoping that my journey and approach will help others who can benefit from the lessons I gained through a lot of trial and a good number of errors. Heck, this is the book I wish someone had given me when I was younger—when I was embarking on my career, when I got married, when I had kids, and when I was trying to grow my career and rise in the ranks. Self-awareness really has unlocked the best I have to offer both myself and others, and while we all have trials and tribulations to navigate, it's the way we approach both them and ourselves that makes us stronger, wiser, and more capable on the other side of them. Just know that you are your own greatest investment. The key, however, is that you have to be willing to *make* that investment in order for it to pay dividends.

Self-awareness ebbs and flows. There are points in time when we have obvious self-awareness, and there are also points when we actively suppress it for one reason or another. Perhaps ironically, my previous level of self-awareness fought my desire to write this book...for years. I wasn't being honest about my fears, and let's face it, we all fear something (if not a few things). When you are someone who operates primarily behind the scenes, and I am one of those people, putting all the details of your most challenging seasons out there can be frightening. I can control a presentation; I'm the one talking, and I can stay in my comfort zone by controlling the narrative. But, when releasing a book, one doesn't have nearly the same level of control over the reactions or the comments or the potential criticism on a much larger scale.

While I was in the most significant part of my own self-awareness-honing process, each challenge I encountered was like a curious fork in the road or an entertaining Choose Your Own Adventure book. One choice typically took me down a road where I'd get to the end and say, "I thought this would be easier; what was I thinking?" (a question that often marks our push-through-or-quit breaking point), while the other choice landed me in a place where I wondered, "Why did it take me so long to do this? It wasn't as challenging as I expected!" Believe it or not, both paths spoke at once when it came to writing a book. There have been moments when I've asked, "Why am I doing this?" and yet there has also been a sense of calm during moments when I was able to catch the reflections of where I've been, where I am, and where I'm going. I can also admit that this was one of the easier forks to navigate, as I'd already spent two years going back and forth on the idea. It was time to put up or shut up...for good!

There is a little-known result of self-awareness that tackling this book did unexpectedly open my eyes to. As I mentioned, for years the idea of putting all these words between front and back covers gave me a nails-on-a-chalkboard feeling. I really do prefer to be Wizard-of-Oz-like, working from behind the curtain (that's the introvert in me), not recklessly throwing myself out into the open. While I have had some great people in my life advise, "You should write a book," my mind had no problem parking that idea in the back of the parking garage—on the very bottom floor. Until a few months later when I'd be driving down the road and think to myself, "I think I maybe want to write a book." Interestingly, the idea slowly and subtly became more and more top-of-mind. This trajectory led me to the bonus understanding: my subconscious is capable of driving the ultimate outcome (and so is yours). This realization further opened my mind to what we are truly capable of. I am by no means a psychologist, but I wonder if it's possible to have a self-aware subconscious driving us toward our deepest goals and desires?

The principles and processes outlined in this book came as a result of my own many years lived without a strong sense of self-awareness. They led me to where I am today, a point at which I know unequivocally what works for me and what doesn't. It's taken the last seven years to really narrow down the details of this knowing—especially on the business side.

People are looking for a definitive, universal, formulaic

plan for finding success. Newsflash: there isn't one. Successful software builds depend upon an agile approach, and in the same way, you will have to intentionally and constantly move, shift, and pivot while shooting for and moving toward your own success. There's no simple playbook. Something will most certainly derail you at some point. But, what will get you back on track each and every time is your own self-awareness.

While I continue to grow my understanding of this invaluable quality and the ways to impactfully implement it into my own experience, what I know for sure is that success is not the byproduct of hard work, an overflowing bank account, or a strong business plan—at least not in a vacuum. *Success is a byproduct of self-awareness.* You have to be self-aware enough to know what you need and desire in each area of your life in order to efficiently work toward it. The comparison game has no place in this process. There is no measuring stick to compare yourself to. *You are the measuring stick!* So, stop chasing what you perceive to be life's byproducts, and start investing in and putting the work into you!

While self-awareness seems self-focused for obvious reasons (and is therefore sometimes dismissed as selfish or a lower priority), the increase in my own has led to a result that is far from it. I've been amazed to see my new-found recognition positively impact my understanding of others and, in turn, every area of my life. I have grown more aware of the ways self-reflection gives me insights into other areas of life. When it comes to interacting with others, I have become more cognizant of those times when people are going through their own challenges of having a bad day, pursuing significant self-development, or otherwise being challenged. As you become more aware of yourself, you too will become more aware of others, and that can do nothing but benefit you in each area of your life.

Ready...set...here we go.

CHAPTER 1

A Few Ground Rules

Before we jump into the process of tapping into and honing self-awareness, we need to address a few ground rules so that you can truly unlock all the benefits that will come from being more aware of who you really are. It's easy to say, "I want to accomplish a specific goal" (and becoming more self-aware is certainly an example of a goal you may strive to reach), but are you truly ready to accept the journey you need to undertake in order to reach the desired outcome or destination as efficiently and effectively as possible?

As we get started, I strongly encourage you to accept the following:

LIFE IS HARD

While cliché, the phrase Life is Hard is one of my favorites to discuss. I mean...yes, life *is* hard! It will knock you down from time to time. Sometimes, it will knock you out.

If you've watched any of the *Rocky* movies, there are a few lines that cross my mind nearly every day; they may resonate with you as well.

The first validates one of the most common ways we get stuck. Rocky says to his son:

> *"Let me tell you something you already know. The world ain't all sunshine and rainbows. It's a very mean and nasty place, and I don't care how tough you are, it will beat you to your knees and keep you there permanently if you let it. You, me, or nobody is gonna hit as hard as life."*

He finishes the statement by bringing attention to awareness in terms of what it takes to win (or simply start moving forward) by saying to his son:

> *"But it ain't about how hard ya hit. It's about how hard you can get hit and keep moving forward. How much you can take and keep moving forward. That's how winning is done! Now, if you know what you're worth then go out and get what you're worth. But ya gotta be willing to take the hits and not pointing fingers saying you ain't where you wanna be because of him, or her, or anybody! Cowards do that and that ain't you. You're better than that!"*

The truth delivered by just this one scene speaks to the fact that...wait for it...*life is hard*. But, at times, we perhaps too easily allow the challenges to stop us from moving forward instead of allowing them to enable us to move forward with greater strength of purpose.

Sometimes, when you watch others navigating through their lives easily, seemingly effortlessly, it can be easy to think, "Must be nice to be him" or "She's really got it good" or "I wish I could go through life that easily!" I have news for you: in each case, you are likely only seeing the duck on the surface; you're missing how hard that duck is paddling their legs below the water line to maintain the graceful surface-level movement you are witnessing.

I can speak to this having been both the one watching and the one being watched. I *was* the "It must be nice" guy who occasionally said, longingly, "They make it look so easy." I watched others driving their fancy cars, living in their big homes, traveling frequently, and posting about their acquisition of every new gadget and gizmo available. It all seemed effortless for them. Yet, in just a few years' time, I went from having that perspective to *hearing*, "Must be nice" and "You make it look so easy!" I can, therefore, with complete confidence speak to the notion that anything worth acquiring requires *hard work* under the surface—regardless of how painless it appears to an onlooker. The reality is that under the surface, it's dark, lonely at times, and full of failure. So, when you say, "It must be nice," understand that it *is* nice. The fact that hard work pays off and the fight for every inch has gained momentum in that person's life *is* nice!

While you may be staring at one heck of a big mountain in terms of your goals and dreams, you need to just start climbing. I promise you, the view from the top is more worth the effort than you can imagine from the place you currently stand. But, before you take even that first step, you have to make sure that the mountain you're preparing to climb is the one you actually want to be at the top of.

RELAPSES ARE NORMAL

We are human, so we have to accept that relapses are normal—even to be expected—while we're going through any transformative process. Noticing and moving past them as they come at you will, ironically, require awareness. Without it, you're likely to figure out that you relapsed five months after it happens, which only leads to wasted time. In my experience, the biggest relapses tend to occur in the area of negativity or the "I can't" mentality, which certainly rears its ugly head from time to time. When this happens, I have to as quickly as possible acknowledge what triggered the relapse and then immediately begin to work on overcoming it.

You're never immune to setbacks.
They are—in truth—opportunities, not failures.

Over time and through careful attention, I've learned to be more aware of the signs of relapse as they're setting in. Sometimes, depending on the magnitude of the relapse, the biggest challenge in getting past it is being able to quickly pull enough positivity around me to snuff it out as fast as I would like. That said, I continue to enhance the way I deal with negativity by drawing on the circle of people with whom I talk through the issue at hand, reflect on what's going right versus what's going wrong, and remind myself that the negativity in front of me is nothing compared to the negativity many others are dealing with. I don't waste time shaming myself for encountering a setback. They're normal, no matter the stage of the game you're at. You're never immune to them. And, in truth, they're opportunities, not failures.

We'll talk about this concept more as the book goes on, but more or less, one of my solutions is remaining constantly aware that my issues are minor when compared to those who might not even have a meal today, who live without the many luxuries and opportunities I am so blessed to have. Pulling in gratitude is almost essential when it comes to overcoming negativity. On its own, negativity serves as a set of blinders to the bigger picture and is the first stage of nearly any relapse. Being aware of the things in your life for which you're grateful is of paramount importance when counteracting any relapse.

STAY OFF THE FAILURE BANDWAGON

Don't get on the bandwagon when it comes to what "failure" means. While we have put so much weight on the Failure is Not an Option mentality, I firmly believe that failure needs to be embraced as a source of life's greatest lessons. It's easy to lose sight of the fact that if we aren't failing (with some level of regularity, no less), we aren't truly living!

When I reflect on and classify the failures I've experienced in my own life, I recognize that it's from those failures that my greatest learnings and successes have come. For example, the end of a relationship is often labeled a "failure," but it was from a "failed" long-term relationship that I learned what I wanted in a life-long partner and what were absolute deal-breakers. I discovered the areas where I wasn't willing to compromise and determined that, in my relationships, both people have to put in work in order for a relationship to be healthy.

Some might suggest that failure is in the eyes of the beholder, and it's certainly a concept that many fear rather than embrace. Because I thrive in failure (for me, it means I am pushing my own boundaries), I find myself frequently reminding those around me to celebrate their failures instead of getting hung up on them. My oldest daughter often comes to me and says, "Dad, I failed," and I can't get to a place where this perspective makes sense. Why even bother with it? It's in the moments of "failure" when we can walk through a few important (and perhaps previously unpracticed) steps in order to turn defeat into victory and set the stage for the next attempt.

When my daughter presents me with this statement, I immediately guide her through a few thinking exercises:

- ♦ What did you learn?
- ♦ What would you do differently?
- ♦ Will you try again?
- ♦ Can you see now that you didn't fail—you simply learned how not to repeat the same outcome?

Many say that the destination is the greatest reward, but I kindly disagree. The journey outweighs the destination by a long shot when you take the time to reflect on the growth that comes while getting to the destination. This is why I don't have a reaction one way or another to the word "failure." In fact, I'd be happy to be served a buffet of failure every single day. I have no problem failing. There is only an issue if I fail at the same thing *more* than once.

I feared failure the same way many do. Unfortunately, we are pre-programed to believe that failure is bad. We hear things like, "failure isn't an option" and equate failing with losing. The only time we fail is when we don't press forward by trying something. Once you begin to associate failure with growth, it becomes an empowering concept!

When I look back on my failures, I also see my greatest lessons and moments of personal growth. If I feared failure, I wouldn't have gotten into another relationship. If I feared failure, I wouldn't have left a comfortable career and jumped into a startup. I will say it until I'm a broken record: anything worth doing is going to be hard work and you will meet "failure" every step of the way. Embrace it, run into it, thrive in it, and above all, don't fear it!

In my world, failure occurs only when I take no lesson away from a moment or I repeat a series of choices that didn't work previously without applying any lesson from the previous misstep. I encourage you to embrace failure. You're playing it safe if you aren't failing, and if you are playing it safe, you aren't unlocking your true potential and happiness.

PROFESSIONAL SELF-AWARENESS

We are each capable of change and growth, but change and growth are only healthy and productive when it doesn't cause us to deviate from our core belief system. Because of that, it's critical that we are first clear on our core belief system——in both our professional and our personal lives. My core belief system includes (but is not limited to!) the following:

- ◆ Even though I'm an introvert, I can get on a stage and confidently and energetically speak to hundreds of people about marketing and data. Yet, I struggle speaking about myself in *any* context, as I don't see an exciting story there (hence my reluctance to pen a book on the topic of my own experience).
- ◆ I am able to engage in professional relationships that can, at times, be one-sided and/or temporary, but I cannot commit a lot of time to personal relationships that are consistently and primarily one-sided.
- ◆ I spend more time focusing on actions than words; I believe that people's truth is found in their actions more than in the words they speak.

♦ I value people who come to the table with solutions, not problems. We all can identify problems, that skill is easily acquired and practiced, but there is great value in the ability to present a problem *and* offer up a solution.

♦ If it's not in writing, it's not going to happen. A simple handshake agreement with someone who claims he does business with integrity and ethics can be quite disappointing in the end. While I used to accept "handshake deals," these days I get everything in writing. It makes it easier for both parties in the long run, and it flushes out the truth of your forthcoming journey in a particular situation before you're stuck in a moment of "I know we may have decided that initially, but I'd prefer a different arrangement now" after you've put in the agreed-upon amount of work and made good on the agreed-upon deliverables.

In short, being clear on my core beliefs represents my commitment to myself not to deviate from what makes me...me! It's important to me to be clear on what my core beliefs are from one point in time to the next (because they can change!).

Paramount lessons that led to big shifts in my professional self-awareness happened on two separate occasions. The first occurred in my early twenties. I was on a mission to find a quick way to make money, jumping from job to job (and when I say jumping from job to job, I mean going from working at a pet store to working at a boiler-room-type mortgage company). It wasn't until my late twenties that a mentor advised, "If you are going to switch jobs, make sure it is an upward move, and realize that you'll have to put in more work; there is no easy or quick way." That was when I stopped forcing change or being more or less thoughtless about it and started approaching it with a greater sense of strategy.

Whenever you find yourself going after a bright shiny object, it's important to ask what you're missing in your current life.

Second, when my wife, Kelley, came into my life, she added a component that I was unaware I was both missing and needed: a person who had unconditional belief in me and my abilities. I began taking more of an inventory of myself and what I wanted in my career moving forward. Some of the first steps I took were relevant, while others were a bit misguided. In terms of misguided actions, I'm mostly referring to the action of putting success at the top of my priority list. When I was younger, I chased the shiny stuff because that's what we're often taught to do. We chase the nice car, the big house, the status-bearing title at work. What I learned is that any time you find yourself going after a bright shiny object, it's important to ask yourself what you're missing in your current life—what void you subconsciously believe that "thing" will fill.

It often surprises people to learn that I'm an introvert. I'm a pretty outgoing person, I speak at conferences in front of large groups of people, and I've held several consumer-facing sales roles throughout my career. The truth is that we are each capable of breaking out of our own labels and comfort zones if that's what needs to happen in order for us to reach our highest, truest potential. Self-awareness is a crucial catalyst in this process. Trust me when I say that this didn't come easily for me; it required a lot of work and practice to get comfortable stretching outside my comfort zone. When I was the CEO of a marketing company out of Sacramento, trying to put them on the map, I had to be on social media, the speaking circuit, and otherwise public-facing day to day. Whether or not the introvert in me could do it came down to asking myself, "Am I willing to be uncomfortable?" My answer: "Yes. Because the juice is worth the squeeze."

I learned to accept both what was necessary to succeed outside of my comfort zone *and* who I am (my core). One of my strategies was surrounding myself with extroverted people. We can mold ourselves to be whatever we need to be when we need to be it. I didn't need to be typecast as an introvert because I know I have the ability to be flexible. Additionally, being introverted has helped me in terms of my ability to look at a strategy from a quiet, non-emotional internal state. Overall, the push for me to move outside my comfort zone was born from my desire to move up in my career—and when it came to speaking and otherwise getting outside my comfort zone.

Over the course of the last five years, I've observed people appearing surprised by the fact that I can execute operationally. I generally get thrown into the "innovator/strategy guy" bucket, and many assume that's where the buck stops. When I was running the marketing efforts for two different business units (marketing efforts that came with a multi-million-dollar budget), I'd inherited a gigantic mess. Yet, I kept creating great events, and further, I was creating them under budget. The perception was that I was flying by the seat of the pants and just "getting lucky." I can assure you, neither was the case. I just wasn't talking about the incredible amount of work I was doing behind the scenes both to develop a great plan *and then to execute it.* (Remember the analogy of the duck paddling like mad underwater while it glides gracefully across the surface?)

While this strength of paddling like mad underwater while being perceived as "flying by the seat of my pants" might initially surprise a few people, it also serves as a great learning lesson with regard to the importance of communicating an idea *along with* an execution plan. Some surprises merit self-reflection in terms of whether the surprise should really be a surprise. I realize this statement may come across as a head-scratcher, so let me take a minute to dissect it.

If someone is surprised by an action you took that they should *not* have been surprised by (in your mind), it's an indicator that you need to do some reflection as to why that disconnect exists.

It took me several years to realize that once I understand an objective, I am off to the races. I clearly see the path, and while I'm actively presenting the strategy, solution, or idea, I've already begun executing, at least in my mind. However, when the task is completed, delivered, or solved, I often hear, "You pulled that out of thin air" or the oft-stated "You sure fly by the seat of your pants!" That response was a surprise to me, but it shouldn't have been. Because it was based on the way my peers perceived me.

People tend to judge in a one-dimensional way. We tend to make judgements or assumptions based on the side we most strongly relate to, so if you are someone who can dream and execute simultaneously, people will have a hard time seeing both. A visionary sees in others their forward-thinking skills but not their day-to-day execution. A project manager often sees someone's ability to manage the minute details of a project but not keep the 30,000-foot-level vision top of mind. Many entrepreneurs choose to purchase companies, grow them, and then sell them. They have little-to-no interest in the tedious micro-management of further growth. So, if you are someone who actually performs well in both areas—vision and execution—but you don't actively and consistently communicate the steps and the plan (and then provide updates along the way), some will seem surprised when you actually deliver. If this is how you also approach tasks and you are frustrated by trigger words or phrases such as "You pulled that out of thin air!" it indicates that you may have to *over*-communicate in those areas to ensure that the reality of your approach is resonating with those you regularly interact with.

Various jobs I've had have also added layers to my professional self-awareness over the years. Have you ever been in a situation where you were about to lose (or perhaps even lost) your job, even though you did what you were told to do? I've been in a situation where I followed rules that didn't sit well with me because I believed that doing so would ensure that I didn't lose my job. And then I lost my job anyway. So, in essence, I lost twice: I didn't stay true to my core beliefs *and* I lost my job anyway. This brought me to the realization that If I'm going to lose something in the future, I'll lose it on *my* terms. Playing someone else's game came at a cost to me because I wasn't playing my hand and being myself. This is the kind of scenario that now requires a combination of personal and professional self-awareness.

PERSONAL SELF-AWARENESS

At times, personal and professional self-awareness will of course overlap, but it's still important to consider them as two separate categories. The first big shock to my system—the one that opened my eyes to the importance of personal self-awareness—was the end of the long-term relationship I was in. With no understanding of self to speak of at the time, I quickly lost sight of who I truly was and instead became what others wanted me to be—ironically, just as I'd done throughout the course of the relationship; as it grew over the course of several years, I didn't pay attention to how off course I was getting as a result of constant probing by my partner to be something and someone I wasn't.

Losing myself meant falling back into the role of people pleasing, and not long after the relationship came to an end, I became cognizant of the fact that I really needed to do some self-inventory to discover who I was, what I wanted, and how I would get there. This was the point when the practice of conscious self-awareness *really* got me back on track—and kept me there. When doing the inventory, it became very clear what I wanted and needed for myself, both personally and professionally. I recognized that reaching the desired result required that I first make myself a priority, mentally and physically. I took the journey in bite-size pieces so that I could feel progress; celebrating small wins is a vital part of the process.

I started with the gym. At the time, I was the heaviest I've ever been, and the gym was a place where I could clear my mind while getting myself in better shape. Now, to bring this to the present day, while the voices that are screaming about the importance of working out and eating a perfectly balanced diet have never been louder, I'm very clear about the level of importance this priority presently has in my own life: round is a shape, food tastes really good, and I love meat. End of story.

From there, I had to tackle my confidence, my belief in myself. I had to stop being agreeable and start pushing back on things that didn't align with the direction I knew I needed to go in or the path I needed to walk. For a long time, I'd been the agreeable, go-with-the-flow, path-of-least-resistance guy. I think that arose more from my desire not to deal with what many perceive as conflict, combined with the number of people who love conflict! If you are passionate about something or have life experience in a particular area, it's your duty to challenge strategy and solutions. You just have to do so respectfully. We all bring different optics to our day-to-day lives, and in many cases, we can share our wins and losses to the benefit of a project as a whole, so why bury your head in the sand when you can contribute by respectfully challenging the status quo?

I remember a time when we had a project to build out and launch, and the leadership team wanted to push it to market early. While many kept their heads down or simply went with the new direction, I pushed back by explaining the possible not-so-great outcomes of an early launch. Because it's important to have a solution to present, not merely a push-back, I suggested a couple of alternatives, including a soft launch or small beta launch to prove my suspicion that an early launch could have a negative impact on the brand. Even though the early launch was pushed through in the end, I owed it to myself to challenge leadership based on my experience and my core beliefs. In the end, the project had to be rolled back, and I was given the opportunity to course correct it.

I had to remove negativity and not allow myself to get caught up in the opinions of others when it came to who I wanted to be and what I wanted to do. When it came to my belief in self, I had to push myself to step *way* outside my comfort zone and tackle things that I feared—things like public speaking and elevating my social skills so that I could interact with more people and not be such a loner or appear withdrawn from groups and small talk.

In time, I would come to realize that what was misguided about my approach earlier in life was how lacking I was in an awareness of what truly made *me* happy—regardless of what made someone else happy. The initial reason behind my pursuit of success was to show others who had bet against me that I could do what they believed I couldn't. While a solid motivator in the short term, I credit my current ecosystem for fueling my ability to blaze my own path and be happy as heck with it, regardless of what anyone else has to say about it. I want to be clear that I'm not saying that I don't believe in traditional measures of success such as financial wealth or high-level achievements; they are simply a *byproduct of success*, not proof of it. A tree's success is represented by its overall growth more than its surface beauty. The magic lies in the roots that run deep; feeding, nourishing, and anchoring that majestic tree.

Ending that long-term intimate relationship also forced a breakthrough in my self-awareness as it made clear the importance of looking *inward* to push aside negativity rather than looking outward for validation and reassurance. I was able to focus on what I learned from the experience and how those lessons could positively impact my future growth. The experience also added weight to my belief that the idea that "relationships are 50/50" sets up a false narrative.

While we're on the subject of balance, let me share a little secret on the so-called "50/50 relationship." When it comes to your marriage or romantic partnership, that mindset will quickly lead any relationship into rough waters. Even the greatest relationships are hard work, just as anything worth something to you should be! I cannot drive this point home strongly enough. I am not suggesting that a relationship is hard work in the way you *might* be thinking, so if that's where your mind went, stick with me for a bit.

The reason relationships take work is that there is always an emotional flux in terms of which partner needs more or less on any given day. When you're on an amazing couples-only vacation, the 50/50 paradigm might be more realistic to expect, of course. But otherwise, you might come home one day and tell your spouse or partner that you lost your job, or a family member passed away. In that moment, you require ninety to 100 percent of the relationship's emotional attention. Or, you come home to discover that your spouse had a rough day with the kids, and the pendulum needs to swing to 70/30 in favor of your spouse. Again, relationships aren't dependent upon fairness or equality at all times; they're dependent upon an awareness of the inevitable emotional shifts within them.

There are times the percentage increases more on one side than the other based on life's demands, which I refer to as flexing. A relationship can't sustain a constant shift to only one side. Sometimes, after I've been traveling, I get home and Kelley is exhausted after a long week with the girls. When I get home, it's important to me to say, "Go get a glass of wine and park yourself in the bathtub" so that she can relax a bit. Of course, I too am dog tired; I've been traveling all week! But I need to put my focus on giving her a break. On the flip side, sometimes *I* have a really long day, and even though things may not have gone perfectly in her own day, she can sense that she needs to make my need to talk or vent the priority. The critical key is that neither of us is 100 percent giver or receiver 100 percent of the time. There is a fluid balance in place, and I own how important that is to me in a long-term partnership.

Having my daughters added another breakthrough layer to my self-awareness, causing me to focus more on my core beliefs and rearrange what I deemed to be priorities in my life. My daughters have been such a blessing in terms of my own self-development, and their presence reminds me every day that I have little eyes and ears watching and listening to every move I make.

The first step in this process is getting a bit closer to your own happiness. I realize that this may sound a bit odd, but you really do have to get intimately familiar with what happiness (and unhappiness) looks like to you. If you didn't currently harbor some sense of dissatisfaction or a desire to grow in some aspect of your life, you probably wouldn't be reading this book. We're conditioned to look outward when things aren't going well for us; who dropped the ball? Who said something unkind? The truth is that in order to stretch and excel in all that we do, we have to begin looking inward and putting in the work to unpack those things that are impacting our happiness in one way or another.

CHAPTER 2

Unpacking Your Unhappiness

Is it just me, or do you also feel like, at times, dissatisfaction has a way of snuffing out our joy no matter how much joy we have in our lives? It is almost as though we naturally sabotage our happiness by focusing on why we are *not* happy in any given moment versus why we are happy and what makes that the case. Unfortunately, that approach only leads us down a path where we are, in a sense, hoarding unhappiness instead of unpacking it. The result of that is that you ultimately have to unpack an entire house full of unhappiness instead of just a carry-on bag!

Knowing what I know now, I'd be willing to make a strong bet on something: *you* are the problem with your own happiness. When all is said and done, *you* are the only thing in your way. And, there is a big difference between

being unhappy one day, here and there, and being generally unhappy for long stretches of time. The former is
normal. The latter is completely unnecessary.

If you are someone who tends to hoard unhappiness, I
am confident that you keep it jam-packed in a spare room
with the door shut, hoping never to have to walk into that
room——at least not anytime soon. The one caution I
extend to those who have packed away a lot of their
unhappiness is, the only way to unpack all of your
unhappiness is to unpack that spare room. There is no
reason to be overwhelmed and discouraged by the notion
that you have to get it all unpacked in a weekend. It's like
changing up your eating habits. One day, you substitute a
salad for fries. The next day, you substitute water for your
regular lunch-time soda. You take it one meal at a time,
one corner of the room at a time. You approach it in bite-
size portions. With that approach, you will have eaten the
entire elephant (or cleared out the entire room) without
even realizing it. As I explained when I was laying the
ground rules in Chapter 1, it's going to take hard work and
a willingness to look in the mirror in order to achieve this
new set of skills with which you can unlock your true
potential.

Now, before we can begin to unpack our unhappiness,
we have to actually admit that we aren't happy (even if we
only admit that to ourselves). We have to be able to say,
out loud, "I'm not happy. I choose to fix that. I need to
change myself, my ecosystem, or both."

To be honest, this process still challenges me from time

to time, which is why we all must have a willingness, no matter how hard the topic, to unpack unhappiness when it presents itself. The reality is, there are a few challenges that will crop up and bring your momentum to a complete stop (momentum is going to become an important topic we'll get into in greater detail in Chapter 9). Unhappiness in one area can easily bleed over into or otherwise impact the other areas of your life that are important to you. Let's jump in and unpack the top three areas within which many people claim to have unhappiness: relationships, money, and work.

When unpacking your unhappiness in any of these areas, it's critical to be brutally honest in terms of why you're unhappy, and challenge yourself to come to a happy resolution. Attaining and sustaining happiness requires effort; it won't just miraculously happen while you're running from every relationship, personal or professional, that doesn't make you happy. Sometimes, a bit of honest unpacking will open your eyes to the fact that you actually need to do some self-work in order to bring happiness into your *being* as well as your relationship.

RELATIONSHIPS

Intimate relationships are tricky when it comes to identifying exactly what it is about them that is fueling your unhappiness. I have failed to accept any level of responsibility for my unhappiness several times throughout my life. It's always easier to passive-aggressively declare, "It's me, not you" or just exit altogether instead of putting in the work on oneself in order to generate the happiness you desire. So, now you're probably thinking, "Great, Dan, how do I unpack my unhappiness on this one, given that you just said it's a tricky area?" Well, that's the fun part, so let's get started.

From time to time, I am 100 percent guilty of failing to accept responsibility in my relationship with Kelley, and sometimes for the stupidest reasons, such as being a "right fighter." You know what I mean—that moment when you know you're wrong, but you keep fighting through it anyway, throwing curve balls that aren't even relevant to the conversation because your primary goal is being right!

There was a time a few years back when work was challenging, and my position was on rocky ground because of new leadership. It didn't take much to get me spun up emotionally, and I was arguing with Kelley about some- thing so stupid that I honestly can't even remember what it was. What I do remember is Kelley calling me out in a way that immediately shut me down and made me think. She said, "Honey, your *un*happiness at work isn't what we signed up for. You carry the load and need to be happy with what you do. You need to take a minute and figure out what you need to do to fix that situation, because your unhappiness *isn't* here!"

This was where the brutal honesty that required that I look in the mirror came in. We are always learning, and please remember that there is nothing wrong with making mistakes or failing—as long as you are able to see the lesson that comes from the moment. There are some tough lessons in life for sure, but the toughest will always involve owning our problems and having a willingness to take some level of responsibility for correcting them.

MONEY

Feeling a sense of unhappiness around money is often difficult, especially because this area can easily blur into relationships. It's therefore important to be careful when identifying where the root issue really is—your relationship with a person or your relationship with money.

Your finances need to be on solid ground in order for you to keep moving forward; you can't have a dark cloud hovering over you when you're working to achieve your goals and not have it weigh you down in the long run. Having too much debt, living paycheck to paycheck, and—if you are in a relationship—not having trust and agreed-upon financial boundaries will create unwanted stress and frustration in both the finance *and* the relationship buckets. If you chase status and material things before you're in a position of financial freedom, you may be getting out in front of yourself (putting the cart before the horse) by, for example, buying the flashy thing you know you can't afford, but justifying it by saying, "This purchase will force me to make the money necessary to pay for it." The very idea is kind of funny, as it's a contradiction; if you made the money and invested it instead, you would reap a more solid return. The greatest feeling is knowing you *can* buy it and choosing not to, deciding instead to invest in something that generates additional income.

Unpacking unhappiness around money provides a solid gut punch for a lot of people, mostly because truly unpacking this aspect of life doesn't come easily. You can (and many people do) first attempt every seemingly easy approach there is. Good luck with that. In the end, you will only add to your unhappiness, trust me. If you really want to unpack this area, you are going to have to be willing to get uncharacteristically real with yourself and be equally real in your relationship. Don't pass go; definitely don't collect $200 (that approach may be the one that got you where you currently are!).

Once you've committed to brutal honesty, you have to get clear on the reason why you're hung up on money. Is it because of others, or is it because you want to see what you are truly capable of?

Sidenote: if your answer is, "Because I want to provide a better life for my family and money isn't giving me that option," hang tight; we'll address that shortly. First, you have to get uncharacteristically real with yourself in order to get clear on why you're hung up on money.

If I asked you, without any knowledge of the world in which you live, "Do you make enough money, and are you happy with the work you do?" what would you say? If the answer is yes, what does more money really provide you with? Be honest. If your answer is, "Yes, but I want to push myself in order to see what I am capable of," then get to work and stop simply dreaming about it.

What can you do to add additional revenue to your household income? Can you level up in your role at work? Can you move out of your current role in order to move up? When I had to address this for myself, I approached it with the mindset that every few years I traded in my car and upgraded. Slowly but surely, I went from driving a Geo Metro to driving a Porsche. I knew that those up-level moves were about nothing more than continuing to compete with myself.

WORK

We are all guilty of not believing "It's not me!" (in our personal *and* professional lives). There were a few times early on in my career when I didn't get the job or promotion I wanted, and it was easier to place the blame on the situation, not myself. I remember a few times I applied for promotions and didn't get them. I blamed the people involved and the situation itself for the outcome that wasn't in my favor.

The lesson that helped me realize that the barrier was actually me came when I took a swing at a position I truly believed (probably rightfully so) that I never had a shot at getting. There was a store manager position opening, and the district manager at the time flat-out told me there was no way I would qualify for it. While I appreciated the candid feedback, I said that I at least wanted to go through the interview process to better myself. Believing I had no shot, I went after it like a true underdog. I asked current employees what they needed and wanted from a manager. I researched the market, asked other managers about their wins and losses, and went out into the market to understand how I could best give that store a lift.

When the time came to interview, I presented a 100-day plan, covering every aspect of the business. The plan left no stone unturned. And, a few days after all of the interviews had been completed, I accepted the position of store manager (the one the district manager said there was no way I'd get). Through that experience, I realized that I am the only one responsible for an outcome. Politics and such may come into play, but there is one hard-and-fast rule I grew into through that adventure: leave it all on the table. Win, lose, or draw, have zero regrets about your attempt.

When it comes to your career, you have to fully own your happiness (or lack thereof), and there are some principles you must make peace with from the get-go.

One, the grass isn't always greener. I promise you, when you think that way, meaning that you leave one work environment thinking that surely things are better at another, you are oftentimes only trading one demon for another (and possibly more).

Two, company politics are everywhere. They exist in every environment, even once you're at the top. They exist in the environment as a whole or in your department specifically or with regard to those you do business with.

My all-time favorite phrase to combat company politics (and one I uttered to fight those politics all the time) is, "I am not going to kiss anyone's butt in order to move up." I fought ass-kissing as well as the "yes man" routine for many years, and doing so was actually costly to my growth. Over the years, I realized it wasn't getting me anywhere, and fighting myself internally by digging my heels in on it wasn't getting me any closer to the happiness I craved. What I've learned in this area is fairly simple and straightforward: I play the game—*in as much as it leads to my happiness*. I fight the fights worth fighting, and I let the stupid things go.

When I looked more closely at the reasons why I fought the concept of being a "yes man," I recognized that it was about ego and immaturity more than anything else (and, not coincidentally, one often comes with the other). The biggest lesson I can share from that time is, as I took on leadership roles, I made sure that my team never had to feel like *they* had to kiss anyone's butt or be a "yes man" or a "yes woman." It goes back to being clear about what you can control as you unpack your dissatisfaction and frustration.

Three, you have to play the game to a degree in order to get what you want. Your work ethic alone will only get you so far. This is where learning to appreciate the act of compromise comes into play, which we'll explore further in the next section.

LET THE UNPACKING BEGIN

As you begin unpacking your happiness, you will undoubtedly hit a few obstacles, at which point you will have to determine what you need to do to move forward. The obstacles that tend to catch me up most are those that compel me to unwillingly compromise, understand which low-hanging fruit to stay away from, understand the difference between a void and a filler, get clear about what I am doing and why, and avoid the path of least resistance.

LEARN TO APPRECIATE COMPROMISE

Compromise is such a powerful concept; some people are willing to engage in it, while others are not. I try to always have an open mind in the most challenging of situations and seek a compromise so that my momentum is not hindered. In my younger days, compromise was more of a mere word to me than it was a logical way to move things along. From relationships to work, I made compromises infrequently, as I didn't really comprehend what the term meant beyond "I'm not getting my way" or giving me the perception that I was going against my own belief system.

In my opinion, anyone who says you never have to compromise in order to attain happiness is a fool. We compromise—or sell ourselves—on what we can and can't live with. When it comes to work, I have my own list of what works (pun intended) and what doesn't in order for me to be happy. Overall happiness is, in my world, defined as the ability to be present in my family life, the freedom to work from wherever I want, and the ability to grow and be challenged by any work environment I am in. When I started to unpack these truths—and doing so was not easy by any means—when I focused on what my core critical areas are and recognized that they were solid, the other noise became just that. Now and again, your core may be tested, but I encourage you to stay true to a willingness to compromise when the end justifies the means.

When I was working in sales, seeking promotions and continuing to be passed over, I got a wake-up call. And it was a big one! I went to my manager and asked for candid feedback, and suffice it to say, be careful what you ask for because you just might get it. The feedback was timely and much needed, and it opened my eyes in terms of the ways in which I wasn't doing myself any favors by creating my own false narrative around compromise. That narrative was, as it turned out, more about my resistance to "sucking up" than it was about my desire to move things along. After six months of having a more open mind, listening, and focusing more on getting to a middle ground with my team members, I finally achieved the promotion I'd been after.

On the flip side of this argument, it's easy to over-index—meaning it's easy to drift away from your core values without immediately realizing it—while trying to over-compromise and get lost in deciphering what is a compromise and what is, quite simply, becoming something you are not or accepting something that goes against your core value system. I learned that lesson in a previous long-term personal relationship; I drifted away from who I was in order to try and become what my partner wanted. And, as a result, I've got news for anyone in a relationship: you can *always* be a better version of you, but the core of your being is who you are, and it isn't likely to change. Your core is your core.

You can go into a relationship thinking that you can change the other person, but the real relationships—the ones that stand the test of time—are the ones in which you fall in love with the person who actually stands in front of you, not the person you hope for them to become. I thank God every day for Kelley, as we love each other for who we are while we continue to grow into the best versions of ourselves. We support each other's growth and don't demand or force anything that isn't authentic to who we are at our respective cores.

Perhaps you're thinking, "Dan, you *just* said that we all have to be willing to compromise, and now it sounds like you're contradicting yourself," Let me clarify. If you compromised going in, and your compromise had to do with corporate politics and required that you engage in some butt-kissing, but your happiness was removed in the process, what compromise is left? You have to make the decision that best serves your happiness without it being one of "I am leaving my job in five seconds because I am not happy." Stay focused on your core and compromise in the areas you can live with. You will find one thing to be true if you hone in on it: life is a mixture of day trades and negotiations. You will negotiate with your family daily, make good and bad relationship investments daily, and day-trade in your career in order to reach your big payday. So, if you're going to play the game, do it with happiness versus negativity and frustration.

Put simply, you *have* to know what your primary deal-breakers are in life and in business.

On the personal side, I will not compromise my core beliefs, and I have a "no negativity" policy, and my family comes first. On the professional side, I want to be more than just an employee. I want to build. As a kid, I enjoyed building things with Legos. When it comes to business, I enjoy and thrive in a space where I can help solve problems or build products or processes that help to grow a company. I want to have skin in the game, and I know that you too may want to have skin in the game! One thing I have learned is that it's not given, it's earned. If you aren't starting a company yourself (which gives you the most skin in the game), you have to earn that skin just as the founder or founders had and do. You have to have equal risk in the company's performance.

I have learned over the years that I thrive in environments that operate in an entrepreneurial manner and/or that enable me to absorb lessons and skills that will help me grow. If I have to compromise in a way that's in line with my core values in order to avoid those deal-breakers, I will. If I have to compromise in a way that is *not* in line with my core ethics and values, I simply won't do it. If

I compromise—whether within my core values or not—and can't avoid the deal-breaker, that in and of itself is a deal-breaker!

BEWARE OF LOW-HANGING FRUIT

When unpacking unhappiness, it's easy to get hung up on surface issues and stop there. For example, on the surface you may be unhappy with your weight—a feeling that I can certainly relate to—or believe that the main issue is that your hair isn't long enough.

You then acknowledge that issue as the biggest one and, in response, go to the gym and eat in a healthier way (or buy expensive shampoo designed to make your hair grow faster). But then, after a period of time, you fall back into the same cycle, and weight re-emerges as a component of your unhappiness. In most cases when this happens (specifically related to one's weight), the individual didn't go after the root of the problem. In my case, I was too caught up with what was going on around me to recognize what was really going on *within* me. I wasn't at an unhealthy weight nor was my health in any danger. I simply got caught up with vanity, as we all do from time to time. Once I acknowledged my *what*, I was able to shift my focus to my priorities and where weight loss fell within the scope of that. My *what* was that I wanted to be fit and have more endurance, so I made that a priority in my day-to-day life by incorporating thirty minutes per day of activity.

You know you're well on your way to solid self-awareness when you can acknowledge, "I'm not in good shape" and ask yourself, "Is now the time to fix that?" If the answer is yes, you make it a priority. If the answer is no, you move on to the next thing. If you don't choose one of those responses, all you do is spin in a circle and keep talking the talk that says, "I'll get to it when…" or "I can't get to it right now because…" in order to make yourself feel better about your decision not to do things differently. In the process, you push *away* the self-awareness factor, keeping it suppressed so that you don't have to claim accountability for any of the things going wrong in your life.

I challenge you to go after the weed's root and not just pluck its surface growth. When you only pull out the surface growth, it won't be long before the weed grows back (sometimes bigger and stronger than before!). Instead of going down the path of taking a few more steps and asking ourselves a few more questions in order to get that weed at its root, we instead simply execute without much thought, and that's how we end up getting stuck in an unhealthy loop. We will tackle this further later in the book, but for now I only want to draw your awareness to the way we tend to naturally grab the closest solution—the lowest-hanging fruit—and run with it. By not taking the time to get to the true root of your unhappiness, you will almost inevitably find yourself wallowing in it again before long.

KNOW THE DIFFERENCE BETWEEN VOIDS AND FILLERS

It's important to understand the voids and fillers in our lives because they draw awareness to what we need in order to feel whole. I believe that there is truth to the notion that any void will be replaced by something (and it's not always something that moves one in the direction of his or her goals). I have seen this play out within families; if a parent isn't filling a need for their child, that child will seek it out elsewhere.

Fillers come in hot and heavy when we are met with a crisis or other emotional void. I don't yet have a thorough understanding of why this happens, but I do have a thorough understanding of the fact that voids never completely go away. They only get parked away, and from time to time, we get a reminder of what we've parked and momentarily forgotten about. The voids that I overcame aren't gone, they're parked, there to remain as a reminder of the journey I took.

I was recently speaking with a friend about the concept of voids. After thinking about it for a bit, she hesitantly confided that her biggest current void exists in her relationship with her mother. She knows without a doubt that they have love for one another, but they are simply on two different wavelengths when it comes to the way they live their lives and the perspectives they have on most topics. She describes her mother as someone who needs to be needed and depended on. Given that she (my friend) is very much an independent introvert, it's not hard to imagine the unhealthy way in which this dynamic plays out.

I asked if, as an independent introvert, she believes that her mother is even aware of those times when she truly *does* need her support. She responded that she didn't think her mother likely was aware, and she then added to that the fact that she's probably missed the times when her mom needed her. The void of a maternal figure causes her to invest more into relationships that she believes fills that void in her life—some of her mentors and friends are more nurturing and "motherly," but in a way that sees and respects her strong, independent nature.

What was most interesting, she said, was that she knows that she's held resentment toward her mother for a long time, and she believes that her mother has harbored the same unspoken resentment toward her. Yet, there comes an amazing peace when you simply dig in head-on and acknowledge that there are some situations and dynamics in life that you will get answers to, and there are some to which, no matter how hard you try, you may never get answers or resolution. Interestingly, a strong sense of peace can come from the acceptance of that.

The process of identifying voids and fillers can be challenging. When many people hear, "Where are the voids in your life?" they immediately think about monetary voids. They're simultaneously assuming that money will solve whatever problems may arise, but it's important to remember that there are many things that money can't buy. I define voids as those things that are missing from one's life on an emotional level. For example, did you not have a great relationship with your sister even though you really wanted to, and once you got married, you filled that void by building a great relationship with your sister-in-law?

While a void is recognized as something that is missing—a place where there is a hole in your life—some voids benefit from fillers (as in the sister-in-law example above), while others need no filler. The void simply *is*. It's a sign of self-awareness to be able to differentiate between the two. One of my voids is the loss of my stepdad, who was also my mentor, many years ago. I don't need to fill the void caused by his presence no longer being in my life; it's just a recognized void, and he continues to live on through me via the lessons he taught me, the way I operate in business, and my passion for the automobile industry.

KNOW WHY YOU'RE DOING WHAT YOU'RE DOING

Watching others try to please everyone is not only frustrating, it's exhausting to watch. I spent several years trying to please everyone, and I learned so much in the process that it now frustrates me to watch others navigate this. The big lesson to be learned on the business side when it comes to this is, making people happy by saying yes or delivering something based on their ask tends to provide only a short-term win. The long-term play is to get comfortable *not* being a "yes person" or taking on a project with a "just do it" mentality. You have to bring *you* to the table in order to deliver beyond the required scope. If you look at a project you delivered or a task you completed without investigating the *what* that you are looking to solve and the *why* behind it, you are missing the bigger win and the opportunity to be far more efficient in the long run. I've learned that the *why* and the *what* really open up your clarity when it comes to the root challenge you need to solve or deliver on. We tend to overcomplicate or further build on something that was broken from the start, which is nothing more than an exercise in futility.

Everyone focuses on the *why,* when the aspect we need to be focusing on is the *what*!

Denial takes us to a place of asking why in the sense of "Why me? Why this? Why now?" When we do this, we aren't asking from a place of curiosity; we're asking from a place of self-pity and getting hung up in the past—a past we cannot change. Going from the *why* of pity to the *what* of purpose will shift you from incapacitating denial to action with purpose.

When people do things in their personal or professional lives that I know won't turn out well, I do my best to recognize that each person has to walk their own path. Watching them do so simply reminds me of a path I once walked (and sometimes still stumble back onto).

We live in a highly judgmental society, and it's hindering change, or better yet, the freedom to be ourselves. If you tend to judge others' paths and choices, get back to judging *yourself,* because honestly, that's what you're doing. You simply aren't wanting to come to terms with what you need to be investing your own energy into.

It's easy to point out flaws in others; it's a whole lot harder to look in the mirror and call yourself out. While it might be a bit (or a lot) painful, I challenge you to do it. It will open up doors you weren't even aware existed.

AVOID THE PATH OF LEAST RESISTANCE

Before I go outward in order to unpack my own unhappiness, I go inward. By default, we want to find the path of least resistance when it comes to why something isn't working or why we're stuck in a rut, and that path involves writing off dissatisfaction by professing, "It's them" or, "It's the fault of the situation, which can't be changed." The path of least resistance is what causes us to grab the lowest-hanging fruit; it's simply easier. We can rationalize and justify almost anything in order to feel better about ourselves, but it's when we dig deep that we uncover the real truth.

Having worked with automotive dealerships for so long, I see a common theme: the dealerships that focus on providing the best internal customer service automatically provide the best customer service to the public. It doesn't work the other way around, however. You can't focus on providing great service to customers coming into the dealership and expect that, by default, you will then provide the same high level of service to those who work there. It simply doesn't work that way. Inward, then outward. Whether you're talking about a company's performance or your own happiness, the formula is the same.

After running into some of the same challenges again

and again over the years, I have learned to internalize, to look inward in order to assess why, what, and how something happened or how I ended up feeling a certain way. I have to honestly address whether or not I am the cause (or at least a part of it). The majority of the time, if we are being honest with ourselves, we *are,* in fact, part of the problem. Or, we are hyper-focused on something over which we have zero control. If you enjoy banging your head against the wall, keep trying to force a square peg into a round hole. Otherwise, figure out a solution or acknowledge that you have zero control over the situation (which is, in fact, a solution in and of itself).

One approach that has helped me navigate things I can't control—one that keeps me from simply throwing my hands in the air and yelling, "I can't change other people!" or "I can't do anything about this situation at a foundational level!"—is using the influence I *do* have instead of needing to be the obvious driver of change and losing out on the ideal outcome. Sometimes, the path of long-term transformation (but not of least resistance) involves asking yourself, "Do I need this idea to be credited to me, or do I just want to help move the needle?"

Just recently, I had a big dose of self-awareness served up over a phrase I used to say because it offered a low-resistance path: "I have no ego in this." Which was a problem, because I do. And, when partnered with the I-can't-do-anything-about-it attitude, it can be extremely dangerous.

I started unpacking both my ego and my pride as I was addressing some dissatisfaction in my business life. I was having frustrations around not being involved in the day-to-day minutiae of the business, and while I said I had no ego in it, I most certainly did; it was just masked as pride. Let's just say I gave myself a big punch in the gut when I unmasked that hidden ego! I had to come to terms with the reality that the company we had sold was no longer mine, and suddenly, I was "just an employee." That's the price of admission when it comes to selling a company, and I had to swallow that horse pill and make peace with the outcome.

Going with the path of least resistance causes you to grab the wrong lever—the one that says, "I quit." When things get tough, it's easy to pull the ejection cord and kiss a particular challenge, task, or goal goodbye. As I look at what much of society is teaching us these days, I recognize that it often tells us to point blame at something other than ourselves and quit when the going gets tough, which is unfortunate.

I find great examples of the quit mentality in Hollywood. Look at the divorce rate there and the underlying message it sends. If you aren't happy, just quit! That's the short narrative, of course, as it's all one sees. One could assume that their unhappiness is based in their relationship and pull that lever, only to find out that *they* are the unhappy one, and they were therefore the one who caused the relationship harm. If you don't have the willingness to commit to a relationship, meaning a willingness to put in work and effort, the path to unhappiness is certain—and when you arrive there, you will be the only one to blame.

Words matter, and at times, we step on our own tongues and elevate situations or get caught off guard when our word choice derails a conversation. I would classify these words as ownership words or accountability words and phrases. Examples are "I am clearly not framing this correctly. Can we restart?" and "I misstepped with my words; may I re-clarify what I am trying to say?" In a world where it's easy to offend someone or derail a conversation, it's important to understand how to own your words and diffuse and reset a conversation in an effort to keep moving forward.

***

There have been moments when I know I pulled the wrong lever. I wasn't being aware of or real with myself regarding the fact that I wasn't putting in the effort I needed to be putting in. As I look back on my early days of dating, it's funny to think about how hard I worked to get into a relationship, but once I won a girl over, it was as though I went on cruise control. Then, things would get rocky and I wouldn't accept any responsibility for its failure. I had this same approach early in my career as well, and it's fun to look back at the parallels between the two. What I learned over time, which has greatly contributed to the way I look at it today, is very simple: if it was worth the fight to get, it's worth ten times that to keep it. I know this to be true, as my marriage is built on this philosophy, as is my career. I truly believe that the silver bullet we are looking for is also the one we don't want to face. We look for a silver bullet or magic pill, as it's generally referenced, to make something easier to obtain or achieve. On the flip side, we don't want to face the fact that anything worth having requires work. This seems to be a widespread problem today; we have lost interest in putting in the work in favor of a supposed silver bullet.

I know that the thought of having to constantly work on the things that are important to you might at first sound crazy, but think about your expectations! I would bet that you want an amazing life full of success and possibly an amazing partner to share it with. If you take those two variables and understand your expectations for them, you quickly realize that as you grow, you change, and you would expect those areas of your life to change as well. So, coming back to my point, you will always be in a state of work, given that change is inevitable! I speak only from my own experiences from marriage and career, and I can tell you that, I've come to no longer consider it work. I consider it fueling momentum. Every day, whether good or bad, I am fueling my eco-system. That ecosystem is what then fuels me to produce momentum.

Even with regard to this book, someone asked me somewhat recently, "Dan, what are your plans for marketing the book?" At first, I wondered if it was odd that I didn't yet have any. It took a good friend who really knows me to point out the fact that I talk publicly about what I'm doing or what I've done, not what I'm going to do. That made perfect sense; it's why my eco-system is so small and so strong, and why I value it the way I do.

Once you make a decision, don't go back and don't second-guess it. We all have looked back at one time or another and said. "I wish I did..." or "If only I did..." but doing so leads to nowhere, as the past is exactly that: *the past*. Learn from the past, apply it to the future, and live in the now. I am guilty of having expressed each of the above statements over the course or many years. I said, "I wish I went to college," "I wish I made a different career path," and "I wish I put more time into that friendship or family member than I did." But, doing so only took me down a path of regret and stopped me from seeing where I was in that specific moment. Today, I live with no regrets; I wouldn't be where I am, and I wouldn't have the wife and three girls that I was meant to have, if I had followed a different path. Every day you are going to be faced with decisions, and you are going to get it "wrong" now and again. Don't lose sight of the lesson, and don't be blinded by second guessing or regret!

When faced with hard decisions, I weigh what the impact on my ecosystem will be if I check the box. I then look at what the impact will be (in other words, what I might regret) if I don't do it as well as what might I regret if I *do* do it. Once I make the decision, I move forward. If there is a perceived negative downstream impact, I am never afraid to simply walk away; I don't want to throw off my ecosystem with a negative impact.

When you're feeling a sense of dissatisfaction in an area of your life or with a situation you encounter, first unpack it. All of it. What exactly are you dissatisfied with? Is it a moment or is it a situation that continues to repeat itself? That question is a big one you as you will inevitably experience levels of dissatisfaction from time to time, and you have to accept that. But you don't have to live in it.

Part two is, ask yourself whether or not you have control over your dissatisfaction. Can you fix or overcome what is causing it?

Part three involves asking yourself whether or not it's time to make a change if you can't overcome the dissatisfaction. You have to be really honest with yourself at this point, as one answer involves embarking on a new and possibly unknown journey—one that could give you the happiness you desire *or* a new dissatisfaction. If the latter occurs, the move could end up being a step backward instead of forward. When it comes to moving forward, make decisions that you can live with.

CHAPTER 3

Dive Into Your Ecosystem

O ne thing I have learned over the years is that people are brought in and out of our lives for a reason. Sometimes we seek out a relationship, and
other times we are the ones being sought out by another.
Through that process, we realize that there is often mutual
benefit to be gained—even when we don't see that opportunity initially. There have been times when I saw an
interaction as one that benefited only myself in my quest
for knowledge, but as time went on, the other person
ended up benefitting from my experiences as well.

Over the course of my life, I have had the privilege of
interacting with some amazing people who have helped
shape my business as well as my spiritual mindset. Over
the last five years, I have been able to pay that forward
more than ever, and I attribute that to the fact that I'm
more self-aware. I listen more and provide advice when
I'm asked for it. Given the intensity of social media, none

of us are short on others' opinions and advice. Therefore, when I'm speaking with someone who is in need of some guidance, I focus on listening while looking to them to fully understand the way they would like for me to best support them. Sometimes, an ear to bend is all someone needs.

The two areas about which I'm asked for advice most often are marriage and leadership. The common theme contained in my answers in both areas is a clear awareness of one's goals or purpose. I look to go beyond the typical blanket statements of "I put family first," "I want success," "I want money," "I'm looking for love," and "I need more confidence." As I have learned through my own journey, these are somewhat empty words and concepts we habitually use to quickly deliver an acceptable answer; we sometimes lack the ability or desire to dig any deeper. Depth can be a difficult concept to achieve if we don't have a true awareness of ourselves or what is it that we really want in life (combined with the true desire to put in the work!). That is the one thing that fries me—the thing many self-proclaimed social-media-famous gurus don't sell when they're sprinkling their pixie dust everywhere (I have three girls, so pixie dust and unicorns are quite real in my world). They neglect the most important part of the message, which is "You have to put in the work." Of course you want the silver bullet to your dreams, but the fact of the matter is, you have to put in the work.

Love them or hate them, there are people out there who absolutely have put in the work. Grant Cardone, Gary Vaynerchuk, Oprah Winfrey, Warren Buffett, Tony

Robbins, Daymond John, Tai Lopez, and Dave Ramsey, for starters, have all put in the work, and they don't sugarcoat the fact that they worked hard and were disciplined when it came to achieving their personal and professional goals.

WHAT IS AN ECOSYSTEM

When you look at the basic definition of an ecosystem, you understand it to include all of the living things (plants, animals, and organisms) in a given area, interacting with each other and also with their nonliving environments (weather, earth, sun, soil, climate, and atmosphere). Ecosystems are the foundations of the biosphere, and they determine the health of the entire earth system.

Simply put, an ecosystem is a system that must work in harmony to be healthy, which is why I relate it so frequently to my own life. If my ecosystem is balanced, it propels me to chase and unlock my true potential. If my ecosystem is in turmoil, however, it makes me counterproductive and challenges my ability to stay focused.

My own ecosystem is made up of a few components—or levers, if you will. Those include my marriage, children, family, friends, faith, work, and self. In some way shape or form, we all operate off these levers (or a variation thereof) depending upon the stage of life that we're in. The fun part, if we are being honest and self-aware, is determining how much weight a particular lever holds in our ecosystem. Many spew the cliché statement

"Family comes first." But does it? I have made that same statement myself, and yet when I started to become more self-aware, I realized that what I was saying and what actually was weren't the same. I was chasing that crazy word: success. I wanted to be successful because it's one of the most self-validating labels there is—even when, underneath the surface, the core of what we believe makes it true is as hollow as a straw.

When you really take time to interact with others and deeply listen to them—both their words and their actions—you can clearly see what their levers actually are, regardless of what they say they are. If someone can't wait to retire, they don't love what they do. If someone says their family is their greatest lever but they're at happy hour every night and spend Saturdays watching football with the guys at the nearest sports bar, is their family truly their strongest lever?

Once you identify what you believe to be your strongest values and levers, it's often interesting to assess whether or not the people in your life agree. For many years, while I said that my family was my strongest lever, the fact was that I was going so fast and so hard that I wasn't taking any time to truly look around. I was like a racehorse running with blinders on, and I had to intentionally take them off.

Today, I know that my greatest successes have come from focusing on my ecosystem and taking inventory of myself, what I truly value most, and—most importantly—what (or, more to the point, who) produces the positive energy in my ecosystem. Sometimes it's easy to think, "I did this on my own; I am successful all by myself" or "I can do this on my own." These statements are lacking in awareness, because while you may have won, overcome, made millions, sold a company, or whatever other wow factor you achieved, if you are being honest with yourself, your ecosystem played a role in your ability to make that accomplishment.

WORK/LIFE BALANCE

There is a common phrase in the corporate world right now that I believe is misleading. That phrase is work/life balance. I feel like it's an advertisement for a misleading way of thinking that one can easily balance work and life. In theory, it sounds amazing, but much like when someone waves something in front of you, saying it's free, there's a little voice in your head asks, "Is it really free?" If there is one thing that many leave out of their narrative, one thing that gives back large gains, it's the fact that they did the hard work. There is no surefire get-it-quick or get-fit-quick plan. Doing anything quickly may yield a quick result, but it will fail you in the long term. I chased the get-it-quick program, and not until my late twenties did I become aware of the fact that anything worth something would require hard work. Today, I can say with confidence that putting in the work pays off.

I think we often fall into the trap of what we were pre-programmed to do in life. We were told to go to school, go to college, get a job, start a family, contribute to a 401k, and retire. When you accept that there is no easy way and that for anything to be great it requires that one puts in a great deal of work, then and only then can you step into true self-awareness.

To acquire and maintain balance in anything you do, you first have to come to the point of realization that you are the balance. To use a bank account as an analogy, you may put more into checking than savings now and then, and you may even overdraft on checking here and there, but in the end, you are the sole determinant of the balance in both accounts.

There have been times when my girls have had a sports event or some other activity that impacted my typical workday. To keep my ecosystem in balance, I knew that the hours that I was overdrawing from work in order to be there for my girls would need to be repaid later in order to recalibrate the balance. What I do for a living allows me a level of freedom to work from wherever I am, and while that may not be the case for you, I encourage you to focus on the underlying point and look at your own ecosystem to determine what ability you have to create balance in your world.

When you find yourself having a "must be nice" reaction to the result of someone else's hard work, go to the mirror, look at the person you see staring back at you, and ask him or her, "Is that particular 'must be nice' truly important to me?" If it's not, change your statement from "It must be nice" to "Good for them!" If your response is, "Yes, that would be nice, and I want that," you have to get real with yourself and admit that the only thing stopping you is you! That's where the self-awareness gut punch comes into play: are you willing to look in the mirror and be brutally honest with yourself?

I have fought this gut punch after declaring that I was ready to get into shape, from "find the easy way" to half-assed attempts to get to the gym. One day, I had to be honest and admit to myself, "It's just not a priority at this time." This has significance because I was eating up a lot of time selling myself on taking action, on statements such as "I'll do it tomorrow," and it was impacting my ecosystem. It was consuming my focus and became something I talked about within my ecosystem but never took action on. Therefore, it became nothing more than a disruption to the ecosystem. Own that which is not a priority. Don't make excuses.

Let's get back on track via the principle that you are the balance in your world. A few summers ago, Kelley and I decided we would take the girls on a thirty-day RV trip through California. Even though we were excited to go, work still had to get done and I needed to be present in making memories for and with Kelley and the girls. So, I had to act as the balancer in the equation. Because we'd scheduled activities during the day, I would start my day a few hours before they all woke up. On rest days at the RV sites, I scheduled meetings while we were in Southern California to visit clients. During lunch at amusement parks or other opportunities for downtime, I worked. By doing those things, work was completed (and we had a great overall month with regard to revenue). I was able to visit clients, my girls got my undivided attention, and I will always remember Kelley saying to me one night, "You know what? Work never interfered in our trip, and I know you were 100 percent here!" So now, when we go on family vacations, this is the approach I utilize. And, if you too are someone for whom work doesn't stop, know that work doesn't have to cost you memories with the ones you love.

I think that we sometimes aren't aware of what we are doing or the negative impact we are making by not being the balance. I have learned through my marriage and having three daughters that my being present or not present makes a lasting impression. I spend a large portion of my time on the road for work, and sometimes people find their way to passing judgement or spewing opinions on that fact. Kelley and I have both been asked, "How do you do that? I could never travel and be away from my family!" Or, the one that really fries me is when Kelley gets asked, "Do you ever worry about Dan being away?" The quick-witted side of me wants to say things like, "You clearly have your own security issues," but that doesn't provide value either way. Leave it to my wife, however, to deliver the perfect response: "While Dan may travel, when he is home, he is present." When I reflect on that statement, there are many truths to it. I remember a time when I was home, but I was buried in my phone. If my phone rang, I answered regardless of what was going on around me. Being home every night with my family isn't a "check the box" activity——it's critical to me to be present and engaged in what's going on in my family members' day-to-day experience.

INTERPERSONAL RELATIONSHIPS

Interpersonal relationships are complicated, and sometimes we really don't know how to deal with the drama that may develop within them (or that comes with them to begin with). As an introvert, I seem to have less of an emotional approach to relationships. As I do in many other areas as well, I tend to bucket my relationships into what I consider short-, mid-, and long-term investments. Like any investment, relationships aren't one sided, and I put energy into each and every one of them. Time will dictate which bucket they fall into, and when it's time for me to end my emotional investment.

Short-term relationships are those wherein two people's paths cross for a short period of time and they gain mutual value from one another. When I was going through the end of a long-term relationship many years ago, I focused my energy into going to the gym in order to get back into shape. My boss introduced me to his friend who was a beast in the gym. We started working out together, and for many months we also met for lunch to talk about relationships and where best to focus our respective energies. During that time, I realized that sometimes, even though in your view it may seem as though you are the only benefiting from the relationship, you are actually playing a role in the other person's life as well. While it's been over a decade since I last spoke to him, the last conversation we had was one in which he told me I'd been helping him through some troubled times.

Mid-term relationships are those within which two people's paths cross from time to time during which they continue to gain equal value from one another. In my world, these are the relationships where we are in contact off and on, but when we are together, there are always engaging conversations and a mutual interest and willingness in helping and supporting each other.

Long-term relationships are just that—two people gaining value from one another throughout the development of a lifelong relationship. For me, this is where I find my circle of influence, trust, and loyalty. These are the relationships that are unconditional, and they are the ones in which I place the most mental and emotional equity.

CHAPTER 4

Identify Your Levers

When we're asked about our levers, regardless of the verbiage used (levers, values, priorities...) we are preprogrammed to deliver canned responses, as most of us have been given a predefined path to life. So, when people ask us what is important to us, the answer typically lands on a pre-programmed and generic response having to do with family, work, money, success, retirement, or travel.

I've often been asked (and I'm sure you have as well), "Why do you do what you do?" My (canned) answer in the past has been, "To provide for my family; they come first." It did, after all, seem like the most logical answer, and it left little-to-no room for anyone to question my motives, right? Wrong! If you probed deeper, providing for my family was really only a byproduct of my selfish want to be "successful." It wasn't until the last four years when I took a big look inward. My daughters were getting older, the amount of time I was traveling was out of control, and I felt lost when it came to whether or not I was really being true to the statement that "My family is the most important thing to me."

My own biggest lever has always been Kelley. When we found that we were expecting our daughter, Sydney (we didn't know the gender at that point), Kelley and I were both working. Kelley made six figures, and I wasn't making anywhere near that. She had it all together, while I was still learning how to do life.

Her two cats had died, so I got her a dog named Abby. One day, Kelley lovingly set up a playpen for the dog at work, and I thought, "This is just a dog. How is this woman going to be with her own child?" I told her, "When the baby is born, you have an option to work or not. Do whatever you want to do." She surprisingly said that she wanted to go back to work, which surprised the heck out of me. I thought that from the minute the Mama gene turned on, she'd want to stay home with the baby. Her concern, however, was "That's a big spread to cover."

This put me into immediate motion. The goal of covering her salary so that she *could* stay home if she chose to fueled me. It opened my eyes as far as how to achieve the so-called impossible moments we generally don't act on because of self-doubt. What I most learned through the accomplishment of that goal (and I did accomplish it) is that when your heart and mind align, the impossible becomes possible.

There are five key levers that I see again and again.

This by no means suggests that you can't have a lever that is not on this list. These are simply the ones I most commonly encounter that have a deep and lasting impact on one's satisfaction with the life he or she is living.

FAMILY

In order to truly have family as a lever and a key component of my ecosystem, I had to internalize my *whys*. I had to make adjustments in order to ensure that I was truly living in alignment with my beliefs and going all in when it came to having actions that supported my words. I can't stress strongly enough that you are going to trip and fall a lot on this journey, but getting back up every time is a far greater end to those falls than quitting on yourself.

If you claim that family is your *why*, at some point (sooner rather than later) you'll have to ask yourself if, based on your actions, they really are. I asked myself that question, and the answer sucked! Let's be honest, we are all addicted to our phones. How did you feel the last time you forgot yours? Exactly! We live in such a connected and immediate-gratification world that those qualities pour into our family lives. As a parent, I find myself being hypocritical on occasion. While in conversation with my kids, I tell them to disconnect and take a break from the hyper-connectivity. Yet, when they call *me* out, I defend myself, saying it's for work and allowing whatever device I'm using to take priority over my family. When I see families out to dinner together, all looking at their devices, I ask myself if we are connecting as a family or connected to our devices. Let me be clear: I am the worst culprit in our house, so the onus for making a shift and the reflection required to do so are most often on me.

As a result, we have placed some rules and boundaries around our time together as a family to help everyone be present, while maintaining the ability to get work done. But the bigger frustration I experience—and that I know many other dads fear—is the worry that I'll find myself asking later in life, "What did I miss?" If nothing else in this book resonates, I hope that this short paragraph does. Because I have spoken to dads who said, "I wish I had been there for..." and "I wish I was more present when..." Those are words I never want to speak, and I hope no father has to. Make no mistake, I am not throwing rocks; we *all* live in glass houses. I am simply catching my reflection off of my own windows.

We are all quick to declare we are doing this or that for our families, and that our families are number one...but are they? I encourage you to back into that statement for a minute and be brutally honest with your answer by admitting, "I *said* 'family first,' but my actions don't match those words. I'm traveling nonstop and owned by my phone, which shows that they truly aren't the priority that I say they are." I personally backed into the statement by admitting, "If family is one of the levers I draw from, I need to invest in them just as they invest in me." It's easy to say the words society has trained us to say, but it's far more rewarding to start making better investments in your actual levers, whatever they are. Everyone discovers and backs into their levers at different times, but when you start putting more focus on your self-awareness, the outcomes you deeply desire will come to you in ways you never expected.

MENTORS

I have business mentors, spiritual mentors, and a group of trusted confidants within my ecosystem who I'm comfortable bouncing thoughts and ideas off of. There is a lot of truth in the notion that who you surround yourself will make an impact, and this likely isn't anything you haven't heard before, but I can attest to the fact that it's true if you actually apply it! If you want to be a millionaire, surround yourself with millionaires; if you want to be a great parent, surround yourself with people who are great parents. The people and environment you surround yourself with will support you in reaching your desired outcome.

I have had the absolute privilege of being a mentor, and one piece I'm hyper-focused on when I'm asked to be a mentor or asked for advice is asking, "What is your why?" As I have said before, we are pre-programmed with canned responses and, to some extent, surface *whys*, but it's not until we are forced to dig deeper that we realize our *real* why. After I get past "What is it you think I can help you with?" I follow up with "What's your why?" and then continue probing until I get to the root of the individual's *why*—his biggest lever.

It's so important to truly listen to others and intentionally interact with them to see what their values really are, regardless of what they say. We need to do more listening than talking, and while I often fall into the trap of wanting to talk, if you want to have a meaningful connection, it's critical to listen with intent.

Here's a funny story to illustrate that we're on a continuous journey, and we are always learning and growing. For as long as I can remember, I have been asked "What do you want to be when you grow up?" and man, that question always put me into a stuttering mess that I somehow managed to navigate my way out of (not a moment too soon). Not having the answer to a direct question *about me* was incredibly difficult. I'd wonder *Why am I struggling to answer what should be such a simple question?*

Fast forward to this year. I'm forty-three years old, and my great friend Frank Lopes (who wrote the foreword to this book) asked, "So, Danny, what do you want to do when you grow up?" Before I could begin my stuttering answer, he said, "It's okay if you don't know!" I thought, "Hmmm, here we go again!" and opted to respond, "I really don't know!" Funny enough, until I put this story on paper, I didn't give him the answer I'm about to share, specifically to show that self-awareness is a process of continuous growth. My answer is simple: I don't *want* to grow up! I want to live the way I did as a kid to some extent—when my imagination, creativity, fearlessness, and blindness to judgement allowed me to unapologetically have so much untapped potential and freedom.

Another takeaway from this conversation with Frank was the importance of surrounding ourselves with people who know how to bring out the best in us. While Frank asks everyone that same question, he knew his almost immediate delivery of "It's okay if you don't know" was the jab that would get each person to focus on his own internal journey to identify the real answer.

FAITH

Another common lever is faith. No matter your beliefs, faith plays a big hand in keeping you balanced. With all society's noise these days when it comes to faith, it's important to remember that we're talking about *your* faith. As such, you are free to believe in whatever makes you feel complete. I admittedly fought this lever for some time, jumping in and out of various approaches, not really committing to it. I parked it away, thinking it was easy to dismiss what you can't visibly see or measure the impact of. Funny enough, over the last five years I have found myself coming back to faith again and again, and I don't believe that it's simply by coincidence that through paying attention to it and nurturing it, I would feel and see so many changes. My momentum picked up, I felt a renewed sense of calm in high-stress situations, and I really felt a need to give more than I would ever receive. In the last few years since making a commitment to faith, I've realized that it was the missing piece in my ecosystem. Faith delivers a calming effect in chaos and also opens up opportunities that you may never have seen coming.

Because time is the commodity we all want more of, one day I made a personal challenge to both myself and God. I committed to giving up one unplanned hour of my day to whomever, whenever, with the goal of making a difference. Let's just say that since I made that commitment, that hour has been the most rewarding of my day! I have had the privilege of using this time to be a listener for someone who needed an ear, a voice for a husband who had lost his way, a strategist for a professional peer who had hit the proverbial wall, a friend to someone who simply needed a friend, and a mentor to those who needed advice on how to navigate a tricky situation. Through those moments, I realized that we are put on the earth to be more—to do more—than we can ever imagine.

Whatever your faith or belief is, invest in it! I understand that going down the faith or religion path can be tricky, and that is exactly why I am tackling it. My faith has brought me strength throughout my life, and unfortunately, religion has become a topic of such contention because people tend to get hung up on what they stand against more than what they stand for.

What this says to me is that we, as a society, have lost our way when it comes to understanding what it means to be an individual. My faith is *my* faith, and while I am happy to talk about it, I place no judgement on others' faith and beliefs. My faith has certainly wavered every now and then, but it has always been a part of me, and over the past five years, it's continued to grow stronger as I have simultaneously become more aware of the way it impacts my life and my family's life.

Your beliefs are your beliefs, and if you are saying, "Dan, I don't believe in a higher power or organized religion of any sort," I am telling you to find *something* from which you get real inner peace. It could be meditation or some other activity that allows you to reach a calm state. We tend to get hyper-focused on achieving our goals and lose sight of finding our inner peace in high stakes, high pressure, high stress moments.

Walk your own path and allow others to walk theirs; we are put here to love, not judge. If you are struggling with this lever as I once did, find a spiritual mentor who aligns with your beliefs as well as the place where you ultimately want to be. I have had many great mentors in my life, and it wasn't until I found my spiritual mentor that I came to the realization that this was a lever that I was missing.

The reality was that I really didn't *find* my spiritual mentor. Frankly, I had stopped looking, given the fact that I couldn't find someone who could fill that void. I was looking for was someone who would work with me to be better instead of focusing on being broke and/or needing to be fixed. That has been one fundamental challenge and frustration in some scenarios I've found myself in; some people think other people are broken simply because they may not be on their path. Instead, it's important to look at the situation from the point of view that people want to grow and are on a continued journey of growth.

While I initially had asked a few people in mind to fill this role for me, they either didn't have the bandwidth at the time or they didn't want to be that person, which was okay; it just meant I had to be patient.

One day, I felt compelled to ask a specific person if he would be my mentor. He said yes and sent me a book titled *Jesus is Calling.* When I saw the phrase "Enjoying Peace in His Presence" on the cover, I wanted to know more and scheduled some one-on-one time with him. It was through that process that I found another mentor who would help me hone in on my internal peace and deepen my connection to faith.

I've now shared my big levers, and while some or all may resonate with you and/or align with where you are, you might also have some of your own unique levers, and that is great! Now, here's the fun part. Whatever your lever is, I challenge you to back into it. The way to do that is to, first, ask yourself, "Is this really a lever, or is it the byproduct of an action, goal, or outcome I'm looking to achieve?" For example, family is one of my levers. I backed into it through 100 percent commitment to them. My decisions, goals, and focus all evolve around them.

SELF

A fourth common lever when it comes to self-awareness is, somewhat surprisingly perhaps, you! Your ability to go to the mirror, so to speak, and be honest with yourself will solve many of your issues. This has become my go-to lever in my efforts to push myself to unlock my potential. When I say "potential," I don't mean it in the way you may think. I am curious about what my true capability is in terms of being the best husband, father, son, friend, and mentor that I can be. I often wonder *What does "selfless" really look like, and how does it accelerate one's momentum?*

I have pulled on the Self lever so many times, for simpler reasons such as wanting to be in better shape to more complex desires to overcome toxic personal relationships. I think many of us can relate to wanting to be in better shape—to the extent that it consumes us to the point that we don't take any action whatsoever. The amount of time I've spent merely talking about it has eaten up more minutes and hours than actually *doing* it!

I had to finally go to the mirror and get real with myself by asking, "Is this a priority or not?"

At the time, the answer was no. So instead of talking about it all the time and then making excuses for not taking action, I made a choice to put it in the "not right now" bucket and come back to it later.

I believe that many of us would rather do something halfway in order to say we tried instead of admit that it's simply not a priority and focusing on the priorities we *do* have, revisiting others when we choose to move them up on our priority list.

Years ago, when I was ending a long-term personal relationship, it would have been quite easy to have a pity party every single night. And, it didn't hurt that everyone around me would have been glad to help me have one, especially if they'd gone through the end of a similar relationship themselves! This was the first time I went for the Self lever and yanked on it as hard as I could.

I remember it as clear as if it were yesterday. It was 2:30am, and I wasn't sleeping. My TV had died, and it was just me and complete silence. As I lay on the couch with my mind racing, it hit me like a ton of bricks: my world had, in my mind, stopped spinning—and yet *no one else's had!* It was in that very moment that I made the self-adjustment to get back into the rotation of the world and start living like I had never lived before—eyes wide open, no compromise, no apologies for who I was and where I wanted to go. We are never broken—not by any means. We just aren't always being aware of and real with ourselves!

CORE

The fifth lever is core. Your core is the representation of your guiding principles or values, which are yours and yours alone. They serve as your operational foundation, and it's critical that you stay the course in alignment with them!

Let me get right to the point on this one, because I've gotten to the place where my core values drive me every single day, and the result is nothing short of remarkable. By no means am I anywhere near perfect; I still have plenty of room to grow. But, I consistently hold true to a couple of core beliefs. One, be a good human. Two, it's not my place to judge anyone else. As humans, stupid thoughts enter our minds from time to time, but awareness helps us to quickly dismiss them and stay focused on being a good person.

When you pull on this lever, it's by asking yourself, "Can this goal be bought, and if so, at what price and with what currency?" Will the price you will pay be in the challenge, the strength and weight you will have to put behind your efforts? Or will the price you pay be related to your relationship with those in your ecosystem? For example, if we're speaking of integrity as one of your core values, will you waiver if, say, you have an opportunity to make a lot of money but at a significant impact to your integrity? You can't say it's your core belief system if it can be compromised.

I immensely value integrity, and I believe that it's a quality that's far better demonstrated through actions than words. I have heard many cite integrity as one of their guiding values, but it's confusing when their actions don't match up. I have passed up opportunities, relationships, and promotions because they did not align with my core values. I have been told I was stupid for doing so, and my response has always been the same: "I have to be able to put my head on my pillow and sleep at night." Your word is your word, and it has great value when it's met with action. While many core beliefs are easily adopted in theory, when your actions do not meet your words, it's like climbing Mount Everest to get people's trust and belief back.

When you compromise your integrity or lose trust, it often requires an absolutely brutal climb to get it even remotely close to where it once was. I have known individuals who cheated on their partners, and while some walked away from the relationship completely, those who stayed together are experiencing a lifetime's worth of work to repair the damage that was done. I've watched solid, years-long business partnerships shatter in a matter of hours after one person took action that was out of line with his word. Those relationships may be repaired in the sense that people can be cordial to one another in a public setting, but they will never return to the previous state of deep respect and trust.

CHAPTER 5

Get (Real) Clear on Your Goals

When talking with others about their current state of unhappiness, I often hear, "I'm not where I'm supposed to be" and quickly have to ask, "Well, what is your destination?" I follow that up with, "Considering the fact that no one gave you a map, how do you know that you're off course?"

Having clarity on your goals is extremely important, as each and every day will present challenges and opportunities that will test your focus on your desired outcome. You will also need clarity when it comes to what your overall happiness looks like; not having that clarity can quickly fog up the path to your goal. When I set a goal, the goal must be extremely clear, and the outcome I am striving for must be one that has a positive impact on my ecosystem.

When I left the company I had been with for five years

to pursue my goal (one of them, anyway) of going back to work with a startup to build it to the point that it could be acquired, my ecosystem had to be in the right place just as much as I had to be. We easily lose sight of the fact that achievements—good and bad—have both positive and negative effects on our ecosystem. To bring light to just a couple of those effects, those with families lose time with them, and stress on you inevitably impacts those around you. While happiness is defined differently for each of us, I'm referring to it more in the emotional sense. I enjoy being in high-stress situations, so I am able to maintain a happy state during intense times. My unhappy state, if you will, presents itself when I feel like my time is being wasted by meaningless activities or an oversight.

Many of you can likely relate to the displeasure I feel related to the following terms or scenarios: micromanagement, having a meeting about a meeting, lack of ownership of a task, kicking the can around the room, and the blame game. Some will suggest that micromanagement doesn't exist at the top level or when you own your own business, but that's not entirely true. If you report to a board of directors, they can micromanage you. Sometimes, even state regulations can be micromanaging! Almost everyone feels a degree of one of the items listed in their career, but the real question will always be, what can you live with as you're working to achieve the outcomes you desire? It's important to first identify the difference between general unhappiness and daily challenge.

CONSCIOUSLY DEFINE THE OUTCOME

When thinking about defining an outcome, we almost immediately tie that definition to some descriptor of success. This is the point in time when you think you're broken simply because you can't seem to get out of the gates and onto the right path to achieve your goals. I believe that we tend to overthink and procrastinate when it comes to moving forward; we subconsciously wait to identify the perfect path to a rewarding outcome. Well, get ready to be disappointed; that's not how it works! I lost so much time chasing the "get it quick" illusion, being a motivational junkie, all to not execute. I was just waiting until I could build the perfect path to success.

The more I learned about software development, the more strongly the nuances of it resonated with me. A software build is like starting with a big box of Legos. There are endless possibilities, and in some cases, there's no definitive right or wrong way to build something. As someone who loves to build and be creative, it's easy to draw a correlation between my life and software, as I am always developing and growing myself one sprint at a time (in the tech world, a sprint is defined as the amount of time it takes to develop or launch a new software feature).

Realizing that self-development has so many similarities to software development changed the trajectory of my internal growth. It gave me a formula by which I could fully unlock self-awareness. Once I realized that nothing is ever truly perfect, and that in order to build momentum I needed movement, the outcome surprisingly became more rewarding because I was actually executing, not just sitting around thinking about executing!

When we consider any goal that we have talked ourselves into and gotten excited about, we have to be aware that we will also subconsciously talk ourselves out of it. When we do, we have to own our foundational why. Why did we set the goal to begin with, and why are we about to stop pursuing it? This is where overthinking and self-doubt come into play, and we have to challenge ourselves to ask the bigger questions and trust our gut more than anything else.

The first step when it comes to getting really clear on your goals is, know where you're going, and be okay with the answer! If you're going for $1 million per year, that's fine. If you're going for $40,000 per year until you retire at age sixty-five, that is fine as well. But, if you're in the latter category, don't say, "Must be nice" regarding the person who is going for (or has achieved) $1 million per year. Instead, own the fact that your happiness looks different from theirs.

The second step is to stop criticizing others' lifestyles and choices. It's commonplace to spend time criticizing The Rock for (supposedly) not spending much time with his family, or Grant Cardone for being too salesy, or Gary Vaynerchuk for never sleeping. But, keep in mind that the time and energy you're spending on evaluating others' lives is time you're giving away when it comes to improving your own life. Also, in most cases, you aren't evaluating their lives in a positive way to determine how you can get to their level. You're criticizing them in order to justify why you don't want to be there (in other words, why you aren't there).

The third step is to execute and get a win under your belt! In Step One, we get clear on our goals. In Step Two, we shed the negativity and time-suck that results from watching others. In Step Three, we focus on executing and getting some short-term wins under our belt to build momentum to get to our goal.

CLARIFY THE BOXES AND WORK INTO THEM

When it comes to asking the right questions, it's not about merely checking the boxes; it's about being clear on what the boxes actually are. I say this for those who put more focus on completing a task ("checking the box") than understanding why you are completing it. If you are someone who works off a list, checking boxes as you go, this concept is for you. Yes, we enjoy having the sense of accomplishment we get from placing a checkmark by the task we just completed. It's satisfying and rewarding. But when it comes to your life boxes, you have to have solid intention in terms of what those boxes are and determining whether they are the right ones for you.

One of my boxes is time, as that is one thing we are all poor at managing. Think about this: do you ever have enough time? As humans, we are constantly working against time, and at some point, our time here will be up. Over the past ten years, I have had time as one of the boxes that I work off of everyday. Everything I do day-to-day is weighed against this box. It started when I was working for a large corporation and we would have a meeting about the meeting on the meeting (anyone know what I am talking about?). Anyway, I realized that I only had so much time in the day, and I wanted to make sure that my time was focused in more productive ways, from helping my team to getting projects underway and completed. So, when these meetings were called, I would generally ask up front what we were trying to accomplish, what my role was in it, or what the desired outcome was for me being included in the meeting to begin with.

This is what I mean when I refer to working into your boxes. Not only does it involve seeking the real why but it's also assessing what your life checklist includes to ensure that you're living your own life to the fullest at any given point in time.

In my personal life, "checking the box" involves staying disciplined in being present and having intent with all of my relationships. Again, I am by no means perfect. That iPhone sometimes owns me, and when it does, I don't get to check the "personal time" box. Which leads me to say, it's okay if there are times when you swing and miss. Just keep swinging!

When I'm being aware of and honoring my time box, it can get a bit tough from time to time. We each have to make hard choices when it comes to who gets our time. What I mean by that is, we each have to make smart investments with the 1,440 minutes in each day. I have made poor investments in terms of where I placed my time and had to course correct.

A wise person once told me, "Invest in those who invest in you," and that hit me like a ton of bricks. It just clicked! I realized then that my time has to have ROI (Return On Investment), and if I truly value my time box, I have to focus on the negative impacts when it comes to where my time is going in my personal life, just as I do in the business side of my life.

While the approach may sound cold and lacking in emotion, once I started putting a perceived monetary value on activities and relationships in my life, it started to help me make more sense of where I should make better investments. It also made it easier not to let emotions or assumptions take me off my path. For example, it's easy to get hung up on someone's "celebrity" on social media and fail to recognize that they can have no real impact in your world. Or, you might jump into a negative relationship thinking you can turn someone's life around when, in truth, turning around someone else's life is not a good use of time if you are trying to get yourself unstuck!

CHAPTER 6

Get (Real) Clear on What's Keeping You Stuck

Man oh man, have I been stuck a time or two. Each time it happened, I so wanted to place blame for the reason I was stuck on surface elements, because doing so made it easier to avoid the truth! Remember, the critical piece to getting completely clear on what's keeping you stuck is YOU! I've come to realize that any time I was perpetually stuck, *I* was the root cause of it. I allowed myself to stay in a mental and emotional state when I had complete control over *unstucking* myself by getting clear on the fact that I could control the outcome.

There are two simple steps I employ when it comes to overcoming the dreaded feeling of "I'm stuck." In fact, they are two of the seven steps that many of us run from—but must instead run *through*—in order to get ourselves out of whatever situation has us running in wet cement. We often strongly dislike confronting ourselves, but let's just call ourselves out on it already. Being honest with ourselves is the hardest thing to do at times, but it's also the time warp that transports us to the place where we're again performing at our best.

First, we have to acknowledge that we are, in fact, stuck! Meaning, we are keeping ourselves from reaching our potential by putting limits on ourselves, unable to get out of our own way. The example I'll use to illustrate this principle is one in which I found myself stranded in a self-pity party because I didn't like an outcome at work.

Last year, I sold my company, VistaDash. We sold it because we truly believed that it would be a good fit with the company that was interested in purchasing it from us. But, I allowed myself to get stuck in the sale (and stay stuck afterward). I was emotionally connected to the business. Once I sold it; it was no longer mine, and I had to accept that. This is but one of many examples I can speak to, and to be clear, many things can cause you to feel stuck in business relationships as well as personal relationships.

As with the grieving process, when you are stuck (and while you're working to get out of your stuckness) you will embark on an emotional rollercoaster. While I would love to take the credit for the realization of how feeling stuck is similar to going through the seven stages of grief, I have to give it to my wife who, many times, knows me better than

I know myself.

We go through the stages of grief when we lose a loved one or experience a perceived life-altering event such as divorce or some other monumental personal challenge. It wasn't until I went through my last corporate acquisition that Kelley opened my eyes to how often we encounter and move through these seven stages during instances that actually *don't* involve the death or other loss of a person. We mourn so many things that impact our happiness, and it's critical to grieve what we're giving up—even when it's as seemingly benign as a job or a role or a title.

It was in that moment that I realized that the issue of being *stuck* was really one of being hung up in the first stage of grief: shock and denial. In this context, the Seven Stages of Grief become the Seven Stages of Becoming (or, in some cases, unbecoming).

What a "coincidence" that denial is the first stage of both. If we are being self-aware in terms of where we are and the fact that we are mourning an impact to our life, it quickly becomes abundantly clear that we are not truly stuck—we are simply in denial of the fact that we have not acknowledged the *what* of self-pity versus continuing to feed our denial of the *why* of self-pity (more on this in a bit).

We all have emotional responses to things that happen in our days. Traffic is slow; we hit all the red lights on the way to work; we discover that we're missing a key ingredient for dinner. But, sticking with those emotional responses to ourselves and others leads nowhere quickly. Take a minute and think of the last emotional response you or someone else close to you had and consider the outcome of it. Did it lead you to your end goal? Did it have a positive outcome for you and any other person involved? We let emotions get the best of us (and, of course, I'm not saying anything new here), but guess what? We continue to lie to ourselves by carrying on with that approach while expecting a different outcome.

I don't know about you, but I prefer to avoid insanity at each and every turn. Like almost everyone else, I dance with emotions a lot; there is no permanent off switch. But, self-awareness leads to sanity as well as the ability to own your emotions in order to keep yourself on track. Let's unpack this concept further as we explore the seven phases of being stuck.

PHASE 1: SHOCK AND DENIAL

This is the phase during which you recognize that you are stuck. What most people do (and what I used to do) is, get caught up in a loop of professing that "everything is okay" instead of going inward and doing a self-check. Like many, I used to go *outward* and place blame for a problem that I didn't even fully believe I had (denial) on something or someone else. I got caught up in this loop when I sold my company. I was in denial of the fact that the company wasn't mine anymore, and once I suddenly worked for someone else, that person ultimately had the final say in terms of where the business went from there.

It's almost funny how glaringly obvious this became in my own life, and I had no idea how the acquisition of my company would bring this cycle to light and challenge me to work through these seven steps.

Tasha Eurich, author of *Insight: The Surprising Truth About How Others See Us, How We See Ourselves, and Why the Answers Matter More than We Think,* discovered an interesting tidbit while doing research on self-awareness. She discovered that ninety-five percent of those studied *thought* they were self-aware, while only ten to fifteen percent of them actually *were* self-aware. She interpreted this to suggest that around eighty percent of those studied were lying to themselves about lying to themselves!

What needs to happen in order to work our way through the Shock and Denial stage is, we must first identify and acknowledge that we are stuck. There were a couple of key indicators I picked up on that showed me my own "stuckness." I felt frustrated, and I felt a dip in my passion for working on or completing tasks. The effects of this stage often extend into our personal lives as well, and that can serve as the easiest way to identify that you're *in* this phase, as you'll get signals from your family. They'll point out your behavior changes. The question is, will you be receptive to the feedback or the callout? Or, will you find yourself being defensive and feeling even more frustrated?

In order to move past this stage, you must confront yourself. It's easy for any of us to avoid being brutally honest with ourselves from time to time. But I assure you, if you aren't being the best version of you at home and you're getting called out on it, it's a clear indicator that it's time to pump the brakes and look inward to get back to center. It's critical to, as quickly and authentically as possible (remember, we aren't just checking boxes here), reach the point where you can say, "I *feel* stuck, but I am fine. This is just a phase."

When facing denial, identifying it and working through it can be a bit of a trick bag, given that the issue itself is denial! You are going to have to apply a lot of self-awareness, as you'll have to ask yourself (and honestly answer) a few questions in order to flush it out. That said, here are a few approaches that have worked for me.

One, listen more and talk less. People who interact with you on a daily basis will pick up on changes in your behavior and body language. It will be a bit frustrating as you continue to repeat, "I am fine," "It's just a phase; it will pass," and "I am stuck, but I am fine being here." So, if you can check yourself at the door by first picking up on what others are observing, you are one step closer to getting out of this phase.

Two, ask yourself a few questions:

- What brings me joy?
- How can I show up differently tomorrow?

Approach your core group of people and say, "I feel off." Then wait for a response. It will confirm where you are, and if your group listens more than talks, you will start walking yourself through as you listen to your own words.

Once you own where you are now, it's time to transition into thinking about where you need to change or adjust to get the momentum required to get *out* of denial.

PHASE 2: PAIN AND GUILT

In this phase, we ask questions like, "Why me?" and declare, "This sucks!" "I let everyone down" and "I am a failure." As we start to emerge from the state of denial, we are often hit by the pain and guilt of what got us stuck and what we were in denial about. Later on, when we dive into *why* versus *what*, we will learn how to bridge these two stages with a different outlook. That said, the stage of feeling pain or guilt is important in helping us not to repeat the cycle. If you are someone who tends to get hung up on a fear of failure (and/or guilt and shame make you feel like you've failed), this is the point where I'd encourage you to focus on *failing forward* by identifying what choices got you here and how you now feel so that you don't repeat the behavior. You only truly "fail" if you go backward by not learning, repeating the same approach in response to the same problem. You can't get hung up on the past to the point where it prevents you from pursuing the future.

During my company acquisition, I wondered whether we made the right decision to sell. I wondered if I helped or hurt the team by selling the company. The guilt that those two concerns generated set the stage for the next two stages as well as the way I behaved when I was around my family.

Moving through pain and guilt is more about asking yourself *what* is causing you to feel pain and guilt. Then, you transition into pondering what you can do to accept the guilt and ease the pain. In some cases, you might slip back into a self-pity state of thinking that if we feel, we can't make peace. If you find yourself in a "can't let go, can't move on" mental state, all you're doing is sticking yourself into limbo. Oftentimes, it's all too easy to get a bit too comfortable there. So, if you start slipping, pause, circle back to the top, and begin again. Add this one powerful question to help you move along: "Can I change the future, or do I bid farewell to my past?"

Sometimes, the guilt and pain exist because you are trying to seek peace or forgiveness from something or someone who cannot give it. In that circumstance, "Why?" will never be answered. You must simply transition toward what you need to do to move forward in a positive manner.

PHASE 3: ANGER AND BARGAINING

During this stage, which often blurs with Pain and Guilt, it is likely that you will find yourself snapping at others and having an exceptionally—if not uncharacteristically—short fuse. In this moment, you have to start unpacking your frustrations and emotions so that you can start to head into the next stage. Doing so will make it easier to park feelings of depression and get into reflection. A little alone time isn't necessarily a bad thing, so don't get hung up on loneliness as a negative. Instead, focus more on the positive side of taking some by yourself time to reflect on what's happening within you.

Between frustration and so-called anger, I was a real peach, let me tell ya. I found myself short-tempered and frustrated day-in and day-out, which I didn't even realize until I accepted that I was in denial and had to make peace with the acquisition. I had to get back to center and get my momentum running again.

Be careful while in this phase, as anger is not an area you want to hang out in for a long time, given the negative impact is has on not only you but those close to you. Don't try and "play dumb" here either; you know when your fuse is short, and you are snapping at everyone around you. It's important to hone in on a couple of simple steps in order to work through this phase.

First, work through some trigger-related questions:

- ♦ What are you angry about? What is so bad that is causing you to punish the ones you love?
- ♦ Second, ask yourself what you need to change in order not to be angry. Do you need to change your environment? Do you need to change your mental state/perspective?

PHASE 4: DEPRESSION, REFLECTION AND LONELINESS

When you are getting hung up in depression, reflection, and loneliness, the voices in your head will say, "I am the only person this has ever happened to." That is the mantra and firm belief of the person in this stage. You've lost your momentum, so you feel drained and tired. You can't focus, and nothing seems to bring you joy. Start unpacking sooner than later so you can move through these feelings; you want to get into a state of self-reflection more than anything else in order to get through this phase.

For me, this phase was very freeing. It forced me to insist on having a bit of alone time to slow down my mind and reflect. And, when I did, I got clarity on the acquisition and the fact that I was stuck and holding myself back. It was a "me" problem, and I had to work through it.

When it comes to navigating depression, reflection, and loneliness, you will spend a good bit of time focusing on the *what* in order to move through this phase. Some questions I had to pose to myself during this time were "What did I learn?" "What would I do differently another time?" and "At what point could I have pulled in some help?" In order to detach from depression, I had to ask myself questions such as, "What would make me happy?" "What were the wins in this situation?" and "What negativity is keeping me stuck?" These are just a sampling of questions that helped me start to push forward, but I encourage you not to try and fight through any level of depression alone, as it can quickly creep out of control.

Leverage the heck out of your ecosystem so that you can get out of depression's grasp. Depression can send you back to Denial like a bad game of Chutes and Ladders, so surround yourself with a positive environment and a strong ecosystem, and identify and be grateful for as many positives as you can during negative times.

PHASE 5: THE UPWARD TURN

The light at the end of the tunnel starts to brighten up as you hit the upward turn. It's not until after you engage in some reflection that you begin to see that *you* are the one holding you back; you can only control what you can control in any situation. As you begin to head toward the light of day, you will start to feel yourself becoming unstuck from whatever was holding you back.

During my own upward turn, I dealt with my emotions around the acquisition head-on and put more energy into the areas where I had the ability to make an impact.

A couple of exercises that will help you move through this phase are:

- ◆ Ask yourself what you do have control over and put your focus on those areas. This will enable you to make an impact and feel like you are gaining momentum.
- ◆ Separate emotion from logic. Because you are likely still combating emotion, you have to ask yourself if what you're doing or thinking is based on or fueled by emotion, or if you come

from a logical place with a sustainable solution in mind.

PHASE 6: RECONSTRUCTION AND WORKING THROUGH

This is the period during which you reset and start working through the things that got you stuck in the first place. The key phrase here is "work through." This is not a time to get hung up or look backward. We have to stay the course, rebuilding and working through the challenge we are overcoming. We can't go in reverse; all we can change is what lies ahead.

Working through the emotions of the acquisition provided me with a strong framework from which to work through the phases of being stuck. The major upside of having gone through these steps intentionally is that I am more focused and energized to acknowledge the fact that I can make an impact on the areas I want to impact. Also, as long as I continue to grow my awareness to the specific area about which I'm in denial, my momentum won't slow down.

There are four important questions that will help you work through this phase:

- Ask yourself how you can construct a better outcome going forward.
- What went (or is going) well?
- What could go better?
- What did you learn?

The answers to the above questions will likely reveal some common themes that you can apply in the construction of your next approach. Focus most on what you learned; don't get hung up on the negative. Focus on the positive side *of* the negative and how you can quickly identify it in order to be better equipped to address it on the next encounter or go 'round.

PHASE 7: ACCEPTANCE AND HOPE

Once you accept that you are the only reason you're stuck, you begin to have deep hope that you indeed can build (or re-build) the life you want.

As I accepted——or, as I would say, made peace with——the acquisition and got refocused on making an impact, I was able to get back to center. At the end of the day, I realized that the formula is rather simple: make an impact in the areas where you can and don't get bogged down in the areas where you can't.

The unfortunate (yet fortunate) truth is that *you define you*. The world is going to knock you down, but *you* choose whether to get up or stay down. I challenge you to get up and live the best life for you!

There is one key exercise to engage in at this point. You must dust yourself off and get after it again. Hope and acceptance come from taking another stab at the thing you swung at and missed. It's about learning what worked, what didn't work, and applying both to the next time at bat. Even though you may swing and miss, the value of the exercise is rooted in the fact that you'll *always* miss what you don't take a swing at! Hope is living without regret and doing what you fear. As an added bonus, it gives those who are watching the hope they need to take their turn at bat as well.

CHAPTER 7

The Journey of Fear

The meaning of fear has pivoted for me through the years. When I was younger, I feared failure and/or letting people down. I know this will resonate with many, as fear acts as a spastic brake pedal whenever you're working toward your highest potential. So many times, I pumped the brakes on my potential, fearing that I couldn't do something. Or, I surrounded myself with people who would let me know that they believed unequivocally that I couldn't do something!

The funny part is, I didn't break free and decide to take my foot off the brake pedal until I got a wild hair to prove someone wrong. When I was in a bad relationship for many years, I was frequently told that I wasn't good enough and wouldn't amount to anything. Even though I was chasing that buzzword, *success*, I feared failure and having to face the "I told you so" that would surely come with it. When I finally got out of that specific relationship, I was motivated and fueled by sheer anger to prove I was capable of more.

From that point, as I started to achieve small wins, I also started to build confidence, and I shifted my language around fear from What if I fail to What if I don't try? Fear is an instant fail-safe from mental and physical harm, and it's designed to be. I am not dismissing certain fears—I don't think I will ever overcome my fear of spiders, for example—but when it comes to my personal development and growth, I continue to train my brain to fear the loss of not doing something versus the fear of failure that may come from trying it.

After taking some time to consciously reflect on this part of my journey, I realized that it was through the journey of fear that I was able to acknowledge a few important things about myself. First of all, I thrive when the odds are against me. Second, fear can be overcome by changing the way you look at something and the reason you have it. Third, failure actually delivers the greatest wins! It has been from my failures that my greatest wins have come—and, as an added bonus, they've given me the ability not to repeat the same mistakes.

No matter where you are in your journey, it's normal for there to continue to be things that keep you up at night on occasion. A few things that keep me up at night now and then (besides wondering if a spider is crawling around the bedroom) are wondering, Did I miss a breadcrumb? And asking, Am I setting the best example for my daughters?

I realize that the "missing a breadcrumb" statement may have lost you or caused you to think of a scene from Hansel and Gretel, but it's a great analogy that I keep top-of-mind these days. I take the time to ask myself what life may have offered up on any given day that I didn't pay attention to. We are so easily (and frequently) consumed with life challenges that we are sometimes blind to the little breadcrumb trail right in plain sight that can lead us to something greater. Sometimes at night, I wonder what moment I missed during the day while allowing life to consume me.

When it comes to my daughters, I sometimes fear that I am not being the best example in a given moment. Was I exhausted and therefore short-tempered? Did I miss a moment when they needed me to be present? Did I inadvertently dismiss their needs? Or, did I show enough affection to my wife to ensure that the girls see our love for one another versus simply watch two people who are just "getting through life?" Those "fears" keep me up at night because I want my daughters to confidently commit to unlocking their true potential; I don't ever want them to settle. I want to push them—but just enough to get them to the point where their momentum is under their own power, not mine. I believe that it's my duty as a father to show them versus tell them how to live and what it takes to navigate all that life will throw at them.

I greatly benefitted from following breadcrumbs in my recent journey to a new job. While I had a great, well-paying position, it seemed that the crumbs were leading me down a different path. When you take off your blinders, you can start to see those crumbs leading you to your desired outcome. Your gut instincts absolutely play a hand in this as well, so always listen to them. You know what I am talking about—it's that moment when your gut says, "Do it!" but your mind talks you out of it, and just like that, you miss out on an opportunity because you didn't listen to your gut instinct. It's that subconscious self-awareness speaking to you, saying, "Just go for it."

Breadcrumbs led me to my amazing wife, to writing this book, and to leaving a stable, financially rewarding job to join a startup that was eventually sold. In each case, it would have been easy to keep going down the path I was on, but I felt an eerie sense of calm about the bread-crumbs that presented themselves and chose to follow them instead. I turned my focus to "What if I say no and this company has merit and meaning and is in alignment with my goals?" When all is said and done, what is often perceived as "luck" could very well be little more than a solid sense of self-awareness.

Acknowledging the presence of (as well as getting rid of) doubt and fear is so important. When faced with an opportunity outside of my comfort zone, I don't ask myself, "What if something goes wrong?" I instead ask, "What if I don't do it?" That question allows me to re-scope my fear. We fear what we don't know because what we don't know is uncomfortable. Fear is therefore like the comfort food with which we enable ourselves. And we do so for one simple reason: we can't pinpoint our *what* because we are lost in the wrong *what*—what others will think, what others will say, what happens if we fail—instead of what we might miss by not doing it, what door might open or what we might gain.

I quickly identify fear of the unknown as just that and dismiss it so that I can unemotionally assess an opportunity in front of me. When I flip fear around, I ask myself, "If I don't do it, what am I potentially missing?" Anything worth anything is going to push you to a place of "What am I doing?" And, to be clear, everyone experiences those moments. There's no perfectly guaranteed investment. You want a guarantee? I'll give you one that's undeniable: you're going to work your tail off. I love what I do professionally, and yet I still have to do stuff I don't want to do sometimes. Everything takes work.

One of the prevailing fears is that there isn't enough of the positive to go around. The word "enough" can have such an impact on our way of thinking, as it can trigger fear, urgency, greed, freedom, power, and fulfillment. When it comes to the last one (fulfillment), it occasionally signals defeat in the sense that there may not be enough of something available to even merit an attempt. Our narrative around the word "enough" quite simply has to change if we want more from life.

If I may challenge the way we think for a minute, ponder this: if one percent of people have all the money, and you are someone who says, "There is no money to be had" or "I can't make more because there is not enough," one could argue that the one percent simply thought differently. If you really wanted to move that particular needle in your life, all you'd have to do is realize that there is always enough to go around if you're willing to put in the work.

In reality, I don't think you start to move the needle of financial freedom in terms of "enough" until you stop settling for not enough happiness, joy, and love in life. We all have enough distractions (pun intended); if there were ever something we didn't need enough of, it's distractions. They take away from our pursuit of the feelings we truly don't have enough of.

We have to put value and focus on the things that we can never have enough of—time, happiness, love, and freedom. Then and only then can we say, "There is never enough." Personally, I want as much time, happiness, love, and freedom as I can get before this ride is over.

CHAPTER 8

Exchange Why for What

Earlier, we touched on the concept of why versus what. Asking why can cause us to go backward when we are too stuck in the grief of "Why did this happen?" Using a car as an analogy, you want to be careful which gear you put the car into. You want to be in drive, not reverse. When you get stuck in denial, you let your car idle for far too long; you don't shift into drive. Or, you reverse because denial is an easier emotion to navigate—especially if you aren't aware that you are there. Being in denial both allows for and justifies sitting on the couch watching Netflix while crying and stuffing your mouth with a box of twenty-piece nuggets.

THE WHAT VERSUS THE WHY OF PITY

I'm certainly no expert on denial—except in the sense that I'm just some guy who has been there many times, and every now and again the same loop plays itself out in my head. It wasn't until I added a new tool to my toolbelt that I was able to more efficiently work through the dreaded phase of denial. That tool involves analyzing the what versus the why of pity.

For years, when something didn't work in my life, I was the one who was going to make it work, no matter what. But, as I learned, life will teach you that trying to fit a square peg into a round hole can consume far more time and energy than necessary.

These days, when things aren't working in my life, I go through a process I refer to as Bucket the Why. First, I ask whether I am the one causing something not to work, or whether it's the situation and/or the environment. I then ask myself, *In order to overcome this challenge, can I go through it, over it, around it, or under it—or, do I turn around and walk away entirely.* Successfully engaging in this activity requires a critical level of self-awareness, and it's one that can take you in the wrong direction entirely if you're not focusing on what your end goal really is.

When exiting a long-term personal relationship, I had to weigh out the various ways in which I could move forward. There were a number of options available. Emotionally, the first thought I had was, "Never again." I would move through life in a completely self-serving manner, not letting anyone get close to me in order to ensure that history didn't repeat itself. But, as I faced myself in the mirror, I realized that that wasn't who I was, and that result wasn't the one that I wanted. In that moment, clarity became a healing agent, and I recognized that having a focus on improving myself would lead me down the path to connect with the right people and, eventually, to fall in love again.

Life will throw you curveballs, but when you are focused and have a framework for knowing where your destination is and taking action steps toward it, it becomes easier to check and balance your course as you go. Again—and I know I've said this throughout the book, but it bears repeating—anything worth anything will take hard work. There is absolutely no easy way or silver bullet.

I've had a few instances in my career when things weren't working out, and I've had to work through which road I needed to travel. Eight years ago, the company I was working for at the time acquired a new company and aligned it to our business unit. Power struggles quickly became front and center, and an executive from the parent company told me to align myself with the leader from the acquired company, as that would be the best move to progress my own career. So I did. But the leader of the acquired company had a different plan, and his plan didn't include me. They instead hired someone they had an established relationship with to execute in the same exact role that I was in. Because I had more than a clue as to what was happening, I quickly called them out, only to be met with their certain declaration that they would never do such a thing. That wasn't the case, and shortly thereafter, I was told that my position was being eliminated and I would have to find something else.

Instead of leaving the company, I fell back into a

previous role, thanks to a good friend who had been watching this all play out. While staying the course and staying with the company may not have been everyone else's choice were they to find themselves in the same situation, sometimes it's important to be mindful that you are always being watched and tested to see how you will respond in certain scenarios. It was a six-month setback, but I put my head down, went to work, and let it all play out.

As the players from the acquired company fizzled out and left, I was asked to step back in and assist in getting the business back on track. I was told by a few people that my actions spoke volumes; I took one on the chin and kept moving forward toward my ultimate goal. Sometimes, you just have to stay the course, deciding to go around, over, or through a situation instead of ejecting from it entirely. I am certainly not saying never to hit the eject button, but if and when you do, make sure you can do so without regret or compromise in terms of who you are.

You may be wondering, "Okay, Mr. Wise Guy, you got it all figured out. Good for you. But, what does that decision process look like when you're in the thick of it?" When I look back at the times when I have pushed the metaphorical eject button, I've learned that there are several indicators that doing so is the right choice for me.

First, I ask what is best for my family. The answer to that question can be unpacked pretty easily by assessing whether or not the opportunity at hand provides me with the time to be present with my family (time) and whether it allows me to provide and create lasting memories for my family (income).

Second, I ask what is best for me. Funny enough, at forty-three years old I am still learning and evolving, and therefore, what is best for me at any given point in time continues to be a moving target. That said, there is a big factor that comes into play when it comes to staying the course, and it's well represented in the adage "Love what you do and it will never be considered work." It's so very true! I have found that when I stop smiling, it's time to look in the mirror and start unpacking what's happening and why.

When it comes to the environment and culture of the workplace (which are two critical points to contemplate), I consider whether they act as fuel for my happiness. If the environment is built on the practice of micromanagement or it's a check-the-box culture, I know the position will be a short run for me. A check-the-box culture is, by my own definition, a leadership group or organization as a whole that is more focused on checking the box on a task, project, or exercise then weighing out whether it's productive and the best use of time. I don't thrive in that space, and in fact, I become counterproductive within it.

Third, I ask whether I can thrive within the culture of the organization. The concept of culture is a mixed bag of sorts. It can be lumped in with the organization's overall environment or it can reflect ideas that come down from leadership, yet the reality of it in terms of the way it plays out is often different from the way it's expressed in writing, and it's often very much out of employees' control.

For me, culture needs to be empowering and encouraging. It needs to be built on actions, not words. As I'm sure you've experienced, people talk a great game, but it's not until you get a little time to see that their actions don't often align with the words you heard in the beginning that you realize there's an unsustainable mismatch. I'm blessed to be in a good position in life right now where I can weigh my options and continue to have options as I navigate the organizations I work with or for. One thing I know for sure is that the ability to have an entrepreneurial spirit as well as skin in the game are a must for me.

PLAN VERSUS FRAMEWORK

In just about every area of our lives, we tend to place a heavy focus on planning and—in some cases—we even over plan to the point where a slight, unexpected change can be crippling. We then go back through "Why did this happen? It wasn't in the plan!" (grief). At times, attempting to change course or even mildly adjust our course can make us feel like we're up against an immovable force. I battled this for many years before I started to rethink the way I planned. The change in my perspective was once again born from my newfound understanding of agile workflows and development cycles.

I started planning my life by thinking through the framework of "What is the end goal?" and "What is the

Minimum Viable Action that I need to take to start moving toward the end goal?" To use a bit of a sports analogy, think about a football game. A touchdown is the goal. And the team can use the entire field to move the ball toward the end zone; they aren't confined to only one set route that they must execute.

We all must take off our blinders so that we aren't hyper-focused on a certain path. Instead, we need to be hyper-focused on the outcome. This approach allows us to see greater opportunities for creative ways to reach the goal—opportunities we may not have previously seen.

CHAPTER 9

Know Your Limits

Early on in life, we begin to believe that there are limits to what we can accomplish. We aren't born with limiting beliefs, but we begin to become limited from the first time we hear, "Don't do this" or "Stay away from that." In youth, we have a wide-open throttle of creativity and possibility—that is, until we hear those dreaded words: "don't" and "can't."

Some of the limits placed upon us are perfectly fair. For example, don't touch an open flame. That's a limit to which we have to pay attention in order to stay safe. The limits to our creativity, free thinking, and ability to achieve the "impossible," however, are limits society has placed upon us over time. The question is, are you willing to go against the status quo in order to achieve more, to continue being curious, to asking why in the best possible way?

I used to think that I was incapable of buying the house I'm currently living in. I thought never in a million years that I'd be able to purchase a home like this, and I vividly remember struggling to make a solid income and losing my identity to the point where I didn't even know I'd like to live in a house like the one I'm presently in.

As they get older, people's inability to get started with an "impossible" idea is often masked as—among other things—worry that someone else will copy their idea. Um, welcome to the world. Content is being replicated and flat-out stolen every minute of every day. I actually welcome that level of competition because I know that it will bring out the best in me. It raises the limits; it raises the stakes.

If a client wants me to sign an NDA, I will. And if people want to copy what I'm doing, I welcome it. The fact is, you can tap into my idea, but you can't tap into my brain. As far as I'm concerned, if I do something that merits copying, I did something right. Instead of getting bent out of shape about it, I'll stay in my lane—with my audience. That competition might even light a fire under me to double down, but I sure as heck don't quit because of it. I don't want to burn any time getting hung up on negative drama when it takes time away from me doing my best work.

On the other hand, I also often hear, "We can't do that; it's already been done." Those are words I never utter. Instead, I suggest, "Break it down and do it better." There's very little new to create anymore, and there's always going to be something better because there's always going to be someone who has more money, more knowledge, more manpower. Stop chasing the Joneses. Be your own Joneses! Say, "Good for them!" and then go march your own path. Don't copy; innovate. Better the product or service. Improve upon it for your customers and your industry.

People put limits on themselves for many reasons, but one of the most common is that they fear what people will think of them——whether they win or lose. It's important to recognize that you're doing whatever you're doing for you! It's important that you win or lose on your terms. Nine times out of ten, you'll win simply because no one else is willing to go that far outside their own comfort zone.

I remember watching an episode of *Friends* with Kelley one night. Monica and Chandler announced that they didn't want to host (and prepare) Thanksgiving dinner, even though Monica is a trained chef and had cooked it for the group for as long as anyone could remember. Desperate for a solution and knowing her competitive nature, Phoebe suggested that the previous year's dinner wasn't that good anyway. As Monica became offended, Phoebe swooped in with the idea that Monica cook just to prove her wrong——that she try to top what she'd made the previous year, and therefore, be in competition with only herself!

To this suggestion, Monica became more excited to cook a holiday meal than she'd ever been, referring to a competition with herself as "my favorite kind!" She then declared, "Okay, we're doing this." Just like Monica (I mean, not really, but sort of), I like to be my own strongest competition.

BE ABLE TO IDENTIFY WINS AND LOSSES

You can't stay too long at the dance and burn yourself out if the dance you've chosen is not in line with where you are going or what you are trying to accomplish. These days especially, it's easy to get distracted and sucked into things that may look appealing but may also have an empty return or end up being little more than a "Hey, look at me!" exercise. You have to be deeply aware of what is a win versus a loss—for you and you alone.

The most current trend I see is thirty-day (or more) challenges circulating on Facebook. From thirty days of pushups to #75Hard, they all involve a degree of challenge in the interest of personal growth. They also all involve some level of skepticism for onlookers; some will say they are doing the challenge for growth but in reality, they are doing it for attention. I sometimes wonder, if you weren't posting your progress on social media, would you still be doing it? I understand that social media provides you with accountability you might not otherwise have, but what effect will that accountability have once the challenge is over?

The #75Hard Challenge originated with ARETE SYNDICATE founder Andy Frisella, and the goal of the adventure is winning the war against yourself. The seventy-five-day challenge requires that participants drink a gallon of water, engage in two forty-five-minute workouts (one indoor, one outdoor), drink no alcohol, consume no sweets, engage in clean eating, and do thirty minutes per day of reading. If you miss any of those objectives on any given day while you're in the challenge, you have to start over at Day One until you complete all tasks for seventy-five days straight. I have watched this challenge from the sidelines as someone fascinated with social media and the various ways people both act and interact on different platforms.

This particular challenge got my attention because many in my own social media circle jumped in on it. There were a few who really got after it, a few who I could tell incorporated a few more smoke and mirrors in order to get attention, and others who supportively rallied around those serious about completing the challenge. A good friend of mine, who is currently a member of the ARETE SYNDICATE, blew this thing out of the water and finished the last day by doubling all the required tasks as a mental statement unto himself that said, "Look what I can do when I put my mind to it."

The fundamental challenge I have with all of the challenges being pushed and peddled is that most—not all, but most—are founded on either a get-it-quick dream or an extreme short-term undertaking. Both lead the majority of people who participate to a higher number of losses than wins. If the challenge is too easy, there is no true reward (beyond the short-lived social media attention one gets from announcing, "I finished the challenge!"). The end high is temporary at best.

On the other hand, if the challenge is too extreme, many will look at it and say, "Must be nice to complete something like that" or "There is no way I could do that."

We need more small wins, goals we can take little bites out of over time and then look back and say, "Wow, I ate that entire elephant!" We all want an extraordinary life, but first we have to get good at living an ordinary life. Then, an above-ordinary life. Then, an amazing life. Hopefully, if we put in the work and are honest with ourselves along the way, we'll reach that extraordinary life. The best part of it all is that you define what an extraordinary life looks like for you, not slick Johnny trying to sell you on what he believes your dream should be or the challenge by which you should accomplish it!

I see many people "fail" these rigorous challenges because they get sick or an unexpected life event occurs that demands their undivided attention or throws them off course for a day (or longer). Their (often unrecognized) intention is to finish a challenge based on someone else's rules and then claim someone else's definition of success. The lie they are telling themselves in the process is that they aren't successful if they missed one workout over the course of seventy-five days or only completely sixty days of what could arguably be regarded as insanity. There is no consideration given to the fact that they actually succeeded because they did the crazy, brutal challenge—for forty or fifty-three or seventy-four days—a series of tasks that they'd never before completed and that they wouldn't have had they not taken on the challenge. Further, I wonder if, when many of these folks start over at Day One, it occurs to them to modify the challenge (or modify it the first time around, even) to suit their goals. What's their intentional end goal?

I've watched enough people attempt #75Hard to come to believe that those who aren't one percenters will try it and fail. Further, when people jump into a challenge to proclaim how much they have accomplished, I often wonder how they reward their ecosystem for putting up with all the sacrifices they had to make in order to complete the challenge. In the end, you might have won, but who lost in order for that to happen?

IT'S NOT ABOUT THE NUMBERS

The obsession we have over the number of likes, comments, and shares we receive on a social media posts is borderline out of control, and it's yet another dance that people stay in for too long and for the wrong reasons. Instead of wondering how the engagement on your social media posts makes you feel, I wonder about how the numbers in your bank account make you feel!

My point is not that there is anything wrong with exploring or testing platforms in order to increase your reach and influence once you have a clear purpose and plan. If your goal is to help others, that's great. If you want to grow your brand, that's great as well. Whatever your reason for using social media to grow your brand, it has to be bigger than an addiction to a fantasy of celebrity. You must be clear about what you're doing so that you don't get into a time suck that merits zero return on investment. Time is a priceless commodity; spend it wisely.

CHAPTER 10

It's All About Momentum

For so long, the word "success" has meant having lots of money, accomplishing lofty goals, and having a general sense of overall achievement. I have also used the word to define my own accomplishments and, as have many others, thought that success equaled happiness. What I have learned about success is that it's the *byproduct* of one's efforts, and there is an underlying word that has much more impact than the word success. Momentum is a concept few people want to pay attention to because, like self-awareness, it sounds sterile. But once it's stopped, it's a mother to kick back up again! You can't give up on momentum because momentum won't give up on you. It can come from a variety of places: events, people, kids, and sometimes, out of seemingly nowhere!

Momentum is the word that has replaced success for me. The definition of momentum is "force or speed of movement; impetus, as of a physical object or course of events." What I learned when I focused on momentum in my life is that it always has a positive impact, and as momentum slows, that slowing creates or is indicative of challenges that need to be addressed. Momentum moves you forward and pulls in the positive energy that creates more opportunities and synergy with others.

Momentum is an invaluable byproduct of self-awareness.

It's truly not about how fast you go in pursuit of your goal; it's about not stopping while en route.

There are a number of principles to be aware of when it comes to keeping your momentum engaged.

When it comes to getting more out of life, my mantra is Do Moore, Get More. Yes, I had fun with the play on words based on the correlation between my last name, the end goal, and the process I employ to get myself and others to *their* end goal. This formula will lead you to the positive outcome you most greatly desire.

DO MOORE, GET MORE FORMULA

CREATE ALIGNMENT OF HEART AND MIND

Plain and simple, when your heart wants it badly enough, your mind will put it into motion. Whatever your goal, mission, or desired outcome is, if your heart and mind are in alignment with it, you will be unstoppable.

There really is something to the notion of taking

mental ownership and believing that the desired outcome has already happened, to speaking the desired outcome out loud. I used to think that looking in the mirror and saying, "I will..." or "I am..." was a bit corny, but those moments in front of the mirror have forever changed me and what I've been able to accomplish.

As I have already mentioned, writing a book was an endeavor I feared, and for the longest time, my heart and mind were not even close to aligned when it came to taking the leap and getting started. The moment when it all came full circle and my heart and mind aligned, it was "mission accomplished." I wrote a book, inspired by the now-common *why*: a purpose that has opened my eyes to what I can do when I am completely aware, honest, passionate, and focused.

If you want to be the best husband, wife, leader, parent, or friend, you have to believe you can be that with 100 percent conviction. Trust me, I didn't get to where I am by not eventually coming to understand that I had to *own* the outcome I wanted. I was very much aligned in this manner when it came to providing the financial freedom to allow Kelley to have the choice about whether or not to go back to work, selling my company, and being a present father to three amazing girls. I owned it long before I get there in my day-to-day reality.

That alignment of heart and mind is critical in driving your momentum. It's what compelled me to find a way to cover Kelley's six-figure salary so that she could stay home after Sydney was born, and it's what continues to drive me today. When I have such conviction and purpose for whatever I want to accomplish, that conviction and purpose align my heart and mind to the point where they believe the goal to not only be possible but already accomplished. I then simply have to put in the work to bridge the gap between the place where the goal is accomplished in mind and the place where it's accomplished in my physical reality.

My belief, coupled with my desire, and sprinkled with a strong drive of putting in the work makes what I, at one time, may have thought was impossible, possible.

GET BUY-IN AND BELIEF FROM ECOSYSTEM

Because I know that this will likely always be a topic of debate, I am going to spend some time on it in order to paint the best possible picture I can around why buy-in is so important. While you may want to be your own hero and go out and conquer the world all by yourself, you must remember that teamwork helps the dream work. If you are married or in a relationship, having your partner's support and unconditional belief is critical to maintaining your momentum. I am not by any means suggesting that you can't reach your goals on your own, but what I have learned is that both buy-in and belief from one's ecosystem serve as a real accelerator to momentum as well as outcomes.

Human nature tends to look at the surface level instead of digging deeper into what really drives cause and effect. The people we look at in awe generally have people behind them who have fueled their momentum. It may not be a spouse or a best friend. It could be a mentor, a team member, an entire team, or a combination. The bottom line is, ecosystems support life by providing balance during chaos.

Surround yourself with mentors and loved ones who positively lift you up—even when you miss the mark from time to time. Buy-in and positivity are fuel for what sometimes feels like an impossible journey. I have absolutely been part of toxic relationships and pity party groups, but my family has lifted me up even when they thought I was a bit crazy for pursuing the goals I was pursuing. Build an ecosystem that will be honest, listen to you, and push you in support of your goals.

REMOVE THE BRAKES

You will find that there are both positive and negative consequences to the decisions that need to be made in order to keep your momentum charging forward. If there is one thing I most hope that you take from this book, it's this: *Don't let anything or anyone put the brakes on your momentum—unless you are spiraling out of control!*

It's important to identify what is putting the brakes on your momentum when it happens. Many times, we are the ones applying the brakes to our momentum by allowing self-doubt or the perceived or expressed opinions of others to influence us, causing us to believe that we are incapable of doing more. This is, in fact, precisely why I am writing this book—as just some guy who wants to reach those who are stuck, just like I was. Anyone asking, "Why me?" is likely still oblivious to the fact that they are the ones putting the brakes on their momentum.

Momentum serves as the energy you will need to climb the proverbial mountains you will face. When your momentum is slow or slowed down, those mountains become harder and harder to climb. "Okay, well what do I have to be aware of and ready to address so that I don't slow down?" you may ask. Funny enough, the answer is nothing you don't already know. Momentum is most often slowed by self-doubt, family, a spouse or partner, work, peers, lack of awareness, and generally unexpected setbacks. In my opinion, the most significant brake on our momentum comes from family, spouses or partners, and peers (in other words, people).

I know I am about to make a bold statement, but I stand by it. You can go this journey alone and be dialed in on your own self-awareness, but you can't be dialed in on the self-awareness of everyone else who shows up on your journey. There are unhappy people who want to spread their unhappiness and drama in the same way that you want to help everyone gain momentum. You are going to have to make some tough decisions in order to remove negativity from your life, and I know that doing so is easier said than done.

Accept that you will have to cut ties with those things that get in the way of your happiness: people, activities, substances, and negativity as a whole. You will have to face negativity from time to time, of course, but you don't need to hang out with it. You more or less acknowledge it, then get rid of it like a bad prom date, which is funny but not (yet it's true).

I will first tackle the idea of extended (or immediate) family being a momentum-slower, as you're probably wondering, "Okay, how do I just cut family out of the picture?" The goal of removing negativity does not require that you cut something (or someone) out with a knife (which I do not mean literally!). The only time I remove the negativity entirely is when it's impacting my ecosystem. It requires that you manage it or them in such a way that it doesn't put the brakes on your momentum. I deploy effort in this sort of scenario to seek to understand why the person in question wants to put brakes on me.

We have to face the fact that there will be some form of negativity in our day-to-day lives, and we are each going to have to deal with it when it rears its head. That said, you have to make sure it doesn't get past you and impact your ecosystem. If it does, it will throw you *and* your ecosystem out of whack. There have been times when my passion for what I do has gotten to a point where it feels like full-blown work, which then became toxic based on daily politics and frustrations.

As an example, I was brought on to run a digital marketing company, and for a couple of years the momentum and outlook of the company was on a track of steady growth. In the third year, we experienced some turbulence when it came to the owner's support in achieving the next growth spurt. While we were focused on some other projects that didn't pan out, the agency was hyper-focused on going in a different direction than the one we were steadily on. In the final few months, the level of micro-management and disagreements between everyone caused the environment to become toxic for all involved. For myself, it was paralyzing; being boxed into a robotic routine is not how I operate. I know the environments that I thrive in...and the ones that I die in. If you are really committed to self-awareness, you have to discover where you thrive best in order to maintain your passion and happiness! And, by the same argument, perhaps you just want a J.O.B. from which you can one day retire, and that's that. That's your why, and I encourage you to go get it, regardless of what anyone else is saying you "should" have or go after.

Recognize that not all braking is negative, however. Properly applying the brakes to momentum is like enjoying a nice glass of wine you want to sip on to be sure to enjoy it and all of its flavors. When your momentum is in full swing, don't forget to pump the brakes now and again in order to savor the reward for unlocking your potential. Celebrate your losses just as much as your wins with those you love; they played a role in fueling your momentum, and they dealt with and stood by you as you fell down time and time again. It's therefore critical to remember that and to include them in the celebrations of victory.

My strongest-driving momentum—the one I never want brakes to be put on—is going home to my family. I often look around while enjoying my drive home each day.

Many years ago, my stepdad was battling cancer. He called me one day and said, "The mountains have flowers."

I responded, "They've always had flowers!" and he said, "But I've never looked at them. I was always consumed by other things not to take a minute to appreciate what's around me." Ever since, I take the time to intentionally pump the breaks now and then, savoring what's around me while going home to that which fuels me.

USE LEVERS TO PUSH AND PULL ENERGY

Even if you're Captain Amazing, you will, from time to time, get run down, slip into Debbie Downer mode, or full-on want to throw in the towel. When this happens, you have to be able to push and pull on your ecosystem in order to get the energy you need to persevere. Remember, life is a team sport, so surround yourself with people and resources that level you up and stretch you to be the best version of you every day. If you want to be truly happy, make sure that you have the happiest of people in your circle. If you want to accumulate a million dollars, make sure that you have a millionaire in your circle. Don't be scared to surround yourself with people who you perceive to be better or more accomplished. At the end of the day, they're still only human!

Your ecosystem can be used as leverage to keep you moving forward. There are days when I come home feeling a little defeated because something isn't playing out the way I expected. But, coming through that door and being loved on by my three little girls recharges me. Or, my wife lends an ear or acts as the voice of reason when I am being unreasonable. Your levers contribute in so many different ways, and once you are aware of what you need and which lever you need to pull to get it, life becomes easier.

There are several common levers people have in their lives, which we explored in detail in Chapter 4. Perhaps the most critical is people. In order to be most effectively self-aware, you have to seek knowledge from people and have sounding boards who enable you to grow.

I have pulled from *so* many people over the course of my life. Make no mistake, my wife is my everything, as are my daughters. I am also blessed to have a core group of friends, mentors, and peers who I pull from. One piece of advice when it comes to creating a strong core group is, give more than you get (or pull).

If you don't have a mentor or mentors, I encourage you to focus on changing that as soon as possible. Each time I venture through a challenge that requires self-awareness as a critical component of an effective solution, I am reminded of one important aspect of the journey that will be critical in your quest as well: you must have a coach or mentor who can help you when you can't find your way back to center. It goes without saying that we, as humans, are not perfect, which is why life is a team sport. There seems to be a crazy myth going around that you are the only one responsible for achieving your dreams, goals, and/or desires, but I can tell you firsthand that while you are the ultimate one responsible, my greatest wins have come from playing life as a team sport. While I am the author of my own life, I am no fool when it comes to acknowledging the fact that I have had some great trainers and coaches along the way, from my amazing wife to my mentors and friends.

Just recently, I started spinning in circles and couldn't get back on track. A friend of mine who was in town visiting helped quickly get me back to being focused on what I needed to do next. We all lose our way from time to time and need directions back to the main road. In your quest to build momentum, stay humble and realize that your team plays a valuable role in your success. *We* are more powerful than *I*; *we* are wiser than *I*.

AWARENESS OF THE DRIVER

Self-awareness drives momentum. This is a critical point. When you free yourself from the mindset that there must be an easier way and stop wasting time and energy asking, "Why me?" and set aside your fears of failure, you will truly unlock the recognition of self-awareness and start to feel momentum in your life.

We all find that it is easy to come to a complete stop, and we are therefore generally more inclined to stop than anything else. I have identified a couple of approaches that have come together over time to define the way I keep myself on track. In my own experience, there have been two areas that have put the brakes on momentum: one, I would overthink something so thoroughly that I never took action, and two, I feared taking the risk or the action.

Overthinking

We are all human, and as such, we can overthink our way out of almost anything. It's important that we take small bites of the task we are working through. If we simply break down the most daunting issues into little pieces and move forward in small sprints, we will find that we don't as easily become paralyzed by overthinking.

Change the Question

What if I don't? Asking the question in this manner is a more powerful way of weighing the risk of something we fear doing. I used to ask why I *would* do something and concerned myself too much with what others would think or say if I did. When I made the switch away from this line of questioning, it was very liberating because fear of failure was a negative. Asking instead what would happen if I *didn't* do something helped me to focus on the positive and led me down a path of curiosity or stretching myself instead of engaging in a long, drawn-out internal debate.

In the end, I started to focus more on just moving forward versus over-analyzing and wasting time with internal conflict. What I have experienced when it comes to applying myself has been rather remarkable, and I am excited for you to unlock your true potential as well. It will undeniably set you up to become a magnet for opportunities. You'll be exuding the same energy you want to attract. Once that happens, you can't imagine the opportunities that will come your way.

FORWARD MOTION, NOT RESENTMENT

Success is a stagnant word often used to establish status. In truth, it's the *result* of momentum (movement). When you get knocked down, go for that extra inch. A small win is acknowledging that you don't want to stay stuck on comfortably toxic ground. As a species, we are inherently impatient, so acknowledging small wins is key. For example, if you go from earning $13 per hour to $14 per hour or read just ten pages of a book you've been struggling to find time to get to, that's a small win. Be careful of resenting your small wins simply because they weren't as much as you planned for, expected, or watched someone else accomplish. A win is a win, no matter how small, and they all contribute to the final outcome.

REVERENCE FOR HOW FAR YOU'VE COME

Something I observe with frequency is people criticizing themselves for all the things they haven't yet accomplished without giving themselves credit for all that they *have* accomplished (in other words, not celebrating the small daily wins or the bigger past wins). I've certainly been guilty of this myself. I once said to Kelley, "I have nothing to show for all the work I have done," to which she replied, "Are you kidding me?" and proceeded to rattle off all that we have and all of the tangible victories I'd accomplished.

I was simply looking in the wrong direction; I was looking forward, not backward.

While looking backward is an action that's often advised against (after all, we aren't going that way), in terms of noting and celebrating victories and accomplishments, it's critical.

Remember how well things have worked out in the past. Make note of what you have accomplished in your ecosystem overall! Carve out time to go back several months or even years, not just a few days or weeks.

I want to be seen as "just some guy" who's living his best life, one that isn't predefined by the criteria of flying in private jets, driving a Ferrari, or having millions of dollars in the bank. It's defined as caring deeply about my family, pushing myself, and understanding that sometimes, we each get stuck.

But we can also get unstuck. And if I'm "just some guy" living his best life, then what is stopping *you* from getting more out of *your* life? Begin today to celebrate both your wins and your losses more. Be sure to take a minute, hit pause, and let them soak in.

Be Genuine

You must always be willing to grow into the best version of you while remaining committed to being genuine. Within today's social media landscape, millions of people are creating fake versions of themselves, which is the furthest thing from being genuine.

Newsflash: it's okay to show real emotions and be vulnerable. I still have moments when I fear judgement or let thoughts of what other people might think creep into my head, just as you do. But doing so only limits my ability to be the most genuine version of me. Why should the opinions of others shortchange the life I want to live and the person I want to be? Why should you shortchange yourself? You shouldn't!

Being genuine applies to not getting caught up in the act of keeping up with the Joneses or being consumed by greed. Stay humble and true to yourself. If your goal is getting the big money and the lifestyle that goes with it, purchase your toys once you've earned them; don't overextend yourself in advance of that. Doing so will compromise your intent to be genuine. If you are getting ahead of yourself in terms of acquiring more material possessions than you can rightfully afford to, you consider what might lose to your need to have it all right now. Remember, money, fame, and celebrity are all byproducts; being a good, genuine human being should come before it all. In short, don't become what you're not (but what someone else wants you to be). Ensuring that this doesn't happen both requires and will challenge your current level of self-awareness each time the opportunity presents itself.

The easiest—yet most underutilized—moment in our lives is the one when we're expressing a genuine feeling. We tend to get so caught up in the rapid pace, the technology, and not wanting to be vulnerable that we express feelings that aren't 100 percent genuine.

Don't have "Leave it to Beaver" syndrome. In other words, don't create a fake facade by focusing on keeping up with everyone else. I promise, you'll get more out of life by being self-aware enough to be the real you at all times.

STEER CLEAR OF GREED

Greed will always cost you more than you have to give, and it's a short-term game plan. It will cause you to wage a wake of destruction you can never recoup, and you'll likely never even see or feel what it ends up costing you.

I was admittedly Captain Gadget once upon a time. I coveted the latest and greatest version of almost any device. But my mindset has shifted. It became less important to keep up with the Joneses (or, in this case, the Apples) and more important to focus on what I really needed to invest my time and/or money into. It's easy to lose focus and get distracted by sparkly things like a nicer car, the newest phone, or the latest and greatest TV. But, sooner or later, you will realize that you lost sight of the goals you set in motion as you got distracted by those things.

I love it when, each time a new version of the iPhone comes out. everyone clamors to get one (and Instagram themselves with it) before someone else in their circle does. We all know that new phone is going to have problems, so I'll wait and pick up the second (or fourth) iteration of it, thank you very much!

It can sometimes be difficult to tell the difference between a greedy goal and a lofty goal, so let me make it easier. When you are wondering, "Is this greedy?" remind yourself, "My goal is [name your goal]. I've unpacked my unhappiness, and I know what makes me tick. The only thing that is greedy is going for something even though it goes against everything I know I am. If I want something, no matter how big it is, and I'm not compromising my character, it's not greed."

Also, let me be clear that greed is absolutely okay in the areas of love and family; I encourage you to get all that you can in those areas. I'm very greedy when it comes to my family! Outside of that, if it requires a compromise of my levers or my ecosystem, it's a degree of greed that I know I need to steer clear of.

Not to derail the conversation from what I refer to as wants versus goals, but one thing that caught me off guard was having a goal, reaching the ability to acquire it, and then not following through. Yup, you heard me correctly. I went right up to the finish line, but I didn't not cross it. I instead started a new race.

For many years, I wanted a Rolex as some sort of symbolic rite of passage, a reward for accomplishing large feats that I thought I might never attain. But, a shift in thinking at the finish line caused me to choose not to cross it. The first time we were in Capri, Italy, there that Rolex was, in a watch shop, staring right at me. Kelley said, "Get it if you want to!" and I went inside with every intention of crossing the finish line. But I instead walked away.

The second time I considered purchasing the Rolex was when we sold the company. My feeling was, "Yes! I got one across the finish line, and this deserves the reward!" But I again passed on the opportunity. I wondered, "What gives? What is driving this change of heart?" Simply put, I came to realize that I was subconsciously playing a bigger game with myself. It was more about wanting to know that I could purchase the Rolex than actually purchasing it. The fact that I could purchase the watch satisfied the thirst I had.

I also acknowledged that I'd had some help along the way. The goal wasn't attained only by me, and rewarding my ecosystem felt like more of a reward than anything else. So, I planned a couple of big trips with Kelley and with my entire family as a subtle thank you for supporting me on the journey. Traveling to Asia with Kelley and spoiling her for the unconditional support she has given me provided more satisfaction than any watch ever would, and taking our girls to the Bahamas was incredibly satisfying. The four of them are the most treasured members of my ecosystem. These moments really opened my eyes in terms of what we are really chasing and whether or not we are actually aligned with the "right" prize at the end of the day. My legacy looks back at me every day, and my time with them is worth more than any possession I could acquire. Live, love, learn, and lead more in order to get more out of every day.

Remember from Chapter 1, any time you go after a bright shiny object, you have to ask yourself what you're missing in your current life. People do crash diets in order to feel an instant win. They join certain programs because they're looking for the "easy" way to get rich or toned or deeply fulfilled. If it were easy, everyone would do it! From believing you can make a million dollars in a week to spending the day listening (and only listening) to "faux-tivators" (a motivator with no proven track record or indication that they know what they're doing), it's blatantly obvious how susceptible we are as a society to this mindset. In reality, how many different ways can you fast, practice keto, or speed read? People are looking for new solutions because they believe that they failed at the previous one merely because "it wasn't the right solution." Baloney. They didn't fail because they had the wrong approach; they failed because they didn't DO THE WORK! Has anyone else ever wondered if all of these approaches are borderline intended to put us in a perpetual mode of failure? The mantra of anyone with a program trying to impact new participants is, "You've tried this, this, and this. None of it has worked. Because what you need is THIS!"

I'm not discounting the creators of said programs—not the ones who are well-intentioned, anyway. I'm simply saying that there is a reason that that kind of marketing copy works.

Here's a thought process that's a clear indicator that greed has taken over (and not in a good way): "I'm here and I've done the work, so I'm going to hurt my employees by not giving them raises in order to keep the money for myself." Yes, I've heard that belief expressed. More than once. It never works out well long-term.

The new game is "I know I can get it, but do I WANT it?" There is no life hack to being a genuine human being. Don't compromise your integrity in order to get to the next level.

Knowing who you are (and who you're not) will keep you from unknowingly compromising in all areas of your life. Through the years, I have occasionally compromised without realizing it—and occasionally with full awareness. That said, I draw a hard and fast line in the sand when it comes to compromising my integrity. We get one shot at that, and it's hard to recover from compromising it. At the end of the day, you have to be able to put your head on the pillow. I've effortlessly stepped over cold hard cash in order to be able to do so.

BE WILLING TO COMPROMISE

I would argue that with age comes a better awareness of compromise, but perhaps this is a "guy thing." That said, I didn't realize how deeply I compromised who I was many years ago as I adapted to a relationship that demanded that I be someone different. Through that experience, I lost myself on many different levels.

I woke up one morning, alone in a quiet house, looked around, and wondered, "How and why did I let this happen?" I said to myself, "Never again," and much like a house, I began to rebuild and refocus on being me. The real me.

But, at the same time, I have to be real about the fact that life is full of compromises, and that's what makes it interesting. We each have our foundation of morals and beliefs, but every day is full of compromises. Take a typical day, for example. You get up, ready to conquer the day with a plan of what the day will look like and bring. But then, you get to work and have a few unexpected meetings, or your child gets sick, or your spouse has a rough day and needs you. All these things come at us on a daily basis and challenge us to compromise so that our life doesn't end up in turmoil. We have to value the art of compromise, as it adds meaning to our lives, sometimes not in the immediate moment, but certainly over time.

Many of us are attached to our mobile devices, and several studies have not surprisingly concluded that many of us are, in fact, addicted to them. I, like many, depend on my mobile device (and I'm not saying that's a good thing). I was so dependent on my phone, thirsting for who was going to text me or what was going to be posted next, that I was not present in the moment. Sometimes, my wife and girls still get on me for always having it with me and, at times, not being fully present with them. The first few times this happened, the thought of compromising by fully detaching from my device gave me anxiety. But, if I am going to say, "My family comes first," this compromise must be honored. So, a few years ago, we all agreed to a no-device-at-the-dinner-table rule. Also, everyone must be fully present during family trips and events. Fast forward five years, and as I reflect back on this, I note that so many amazing things came from this compromise.

Dinner with my family is amazing. We have so many great conversations. I have used the "no electronics" rule in business meetings more for me than anyone around me, although it was obvious that both I and several others needed that rule. The one benefit I didn't see coming was the impact on my three girls, who are older now and more technologically connected. For them to sit at a dinner table anywhere and be present with those around them has been an eye-opening lesson for me. To see them engage in meaningful conversation and be engaged in human interaction instead of wanting to be heads-down in a device challenged my own way of thinking in terms of where it's most important for me to be present in a given moment.

CHAPTER 12

Value Your Most Precious Commodity

Time is the most precious thing we have—we get only one shot at life—so the number one question always has to be, "Is this worth my time?" Much like a vampire, life will suck you to death, so make the choice to invest your time wisely. Many of us face things that aren't working out the way we had hoped, and trust me when I say that no one is immune to things not working out the way they planned—for better or for worse. I have come to a couple of forks in the road myself that I had to weigh out and make decisions on, both personally and professionally, with regard to what was most worthy of my time.

Time management has been such an interesting topic for many years, and it's a concept constantly discussed in business. You can have the best plan and time management skills on earth, but if life throws you a curveball, have you built a strong enough foundation to stay on course? I break the concept of time management into two buckets to help me prioritize, while allowing me the flexibility to adapt to the curveballs and pivots that life shells out. One is based on a broad baseline (or a loose, baseline goal), and the other is based on a granular baseline (or a tight, focused goal).

The first bucket is Life Management (which is the broad baseline). In this area, I'm clear on my priorities (i.e., family) and have clarity as far as what and who is important. This clarity drives all of my decisions around both life and time management, so I have to be honest with myself in order to stay the course. My family is the driver behind everything I do. I factor in the impacts of time spent away from them, being present with them, what impacts me, and what doesn't allow me to be the best version of myself for them. When making decisions, I weigh out the example I am setting for my girls and ensure that I can explain without any doubt the why behind my choices.

It's important to have a framework (or outline) with a clear destination so that you're not simply wandering aimlessly through life. Some of these destinations are simple in theory, such as, "I want to have financial freedom by the age of forty-eight" and "I want to give my girls the best education and life experiences so that they are ahead later in life."

While it isn't everyone's cup of tea, I like having

contingency plans. Some say they never plan on losing, so they don't waste time creating a back-up plan, but I know who I am and have had that approach burn me, so I build a few failsafes into many of the things I do. Financially, this includes savings and investment accounts. On the work side, it includes keeping the door open to new opportunities that align with my personal goals.

The second bucket is Time Management, and this is the area in which I have a more granular baseline. I manage my time in terms of home (being present), work (where I can make an impact), and personal (self-development).

One of the unique approaches I've taken in my day-to-day time management is, I make sure that I don't pack my schedule full from morning until night. I make sure that there is a free hour in each day, and inevitably, it fills itself. There always comes a point in my day when someone engages who I didn't expect to engage. Somebody says, "Can you help me with this?" or "I could use your advice with something." Once, as I was heading to Starbucks, I saw a homeless man. As I was walking back out to my car, I saw him again and thought it was odd that I passed him twice. So, I took a moment to help him out. The way I see it, I can lose away an hour on social media, or I can make that hour available to make a difference. The latter is more important to me.

Everyone is so quick to fill their schedules, but what are they actually accomplishing? Further, consider the number of times you actually stick to your schedule from the time you wake up until the time you go to bed? Unless you're a unicorn or the best time manager I've ever met (and I've met some good ones), I've yet to see a calendar "go right" on a consistent basis. Meetings start late. They run over. Unplanned hiccups arise. Someone please tell me why we over-index and cripple ourselves to the point of failure all in the name of "having a packed schedule" that somehow makes us successful!

I wake up every day with a framework for the day. I know what I want to accomplish overall. On the last day of the month, for example, my goal is to bring in as much revenue as possible. I know what the mission is. But that's my goal; it isn't necessarily the best goal for everyone else.

I'm all for working backward, reverse-engineering if you will. The challenge, however, is that everyone is trying to get everyone else to create micro-schedules wherein we account for every single minute of every day. There's a notion that we must over-plan in order to reach success. Whose definition of success is even being referenced? What is success? First, let's all just wake up and be grateful we woke up! Make your bed; that allows you to accomplish something right when you wake up.

During the course of the day, if something comes across my desk that isn't in line with the day's goal, I park it for the future. I've gotten up and left meetings because they weren't in line with my daily goal. Meetings are often mandatory even though they don't move the needle in terms of what I'm working on specifically. When it starts to feel like I'm in that situation, I ask those in attendance what we're trying to achieve. If it's simply a feel-out meeting or we're meeting just to meet, I exit stage right. If the meeting's scope includes items I can't contribute to, I also politely excuse myself. Of course I ask a few qualifying questions to ensure that my presence isn't necessary to move the needle forward. When I receive pushback and still am convicted that my presence isn't necessary, I push harder until I ultimately excuse myself...or am (professionally) excused. It's critical that it's clear what challenge the meeting is intended to solve and how I can help. Once it's determined that I can't, I'm out.

I also have an approach that I implement any time bickering and finger pointing start in meetings. There's no finger-pointing allowed. I instead drive the focus to simply agreeing that there is a problem. We then agree on a solution. The meeting is then adjourned, and we execute.

CHAPTER 13

Parrot Syndrome

Recognize when you're being a parrot. And then stop.

When I ask people why they're approaching something a certain way, they often respond with some variation of "So-and-so did it that way, and it worked so..." or "This successful person did it this way so that must be the right way." There's a big difference between not re-inventing the wheel and mindlessly parroting someone else's approach. It's critical to be able to discern the difference between embarking on an approach in the interest of saving time (not reinventing the wheel) and merely doing something because you perceive it as an approach that will be successful for you as well (or you want the validation that comes with doing something that other "successful" people have done).

It's probably safe to suggest that you are on at least one social media platform, and you have, therefore, more than likely have heard of (and possibly follow) Gary

Vaynerchuk. But if not, choose another "celebrity" you actively follow on social media. With him or her in your head, follow along on this example. There are many people who are trying to replicate (or parrot) Gary. The challenge is that people jump right in and do exactly what he does while expecting the same result. They then wonder why it's not working as well or why people are not engaging with them.

The answer is that, first of all, they never took the time to explore Gary's full backstory in order to understand how he got where he is today. In short, it took a lot of work! Second, they never took the time to assess how their plan aligns with what Gary has done. Third, they didn't clearly declare their desired outcome. That, in my opinion, is the most critical miss for many. They are conflicted over the actual outcome as they get hung up on their addiction to likes and comments. They are focused on engagement, with the desired outcome of growing rich and famous. I use social media for brand awareness and intelligence, and I understand that it indirectly influences lead generation, but I don't get lost in the time suck it can become when you get out of your lane and aren't using it in an intentional, strategic fashion with reasonable goals and timelines.

I am by no means saying that social media doesn't work or is a bad thing. I am simply suggesting that you have a purposeful plan, and stay focused on your desired outcome.

When you parrot someone else's approach without

first assessing whether or not it's truly the best approach for you, you're changing who you are and that is in direct opposition to the importance of being genuine. You have to know who you are and what you're going for and allow that knowledge to serve as the foundation of any approach you undertake.

As an example, people continue to tell me that I should do Facebook lives. I haven't yet done one because everyone else is doing it, and I'm not an everyone-else-is-doing-it kind of guy. I know I don't have to be what everyone else is or do what everyone else is doing. If I'm going to start doing Facebook lives, it will be because it's the right sheet of music for me to play at a particular point in time.

I often hear, "You should follow this person" or "You should study that person." Once you do that without self-awareness (and the authentic intention and purpose that comes with it), you're no longer in control of your own destiny. People seem to forget that we each have to be able to live with the consequences of our choices. If you do what everyone else is doing and it bombs, it's not the fault of the person you copied. Everyone these days is trying to position themselves as an authority, especially on social media platforms, and I think that many are, in fact, using their chosen platforms incorrectly. If you want to generate sales leads, LinkedIn is often a better platform than Facebook from an organic post standpoint, especially in certain industries. If you are educating, coaching, motivating, or storytelling, Facebook is likely the more appropriate platform. When you sift through all the noise, which ones are truly making an impact? Which ones are "successful" in the sense that they've earned the right to do what they're doing?

I did what I was "supposed" to do—what everyone else was doing—and almost lost my job once. Sometimes you are given a framework or direction that may not be in alignment with who you are, and when that happens, I caution you to think it through. You know what feels right for you. Ask yourself a simple question: "If I lose this moment, is it on my terms or someone else's?" Can you live with the answer? If not, it's time to double down on what's driving you.

In short, people parrot because they don't have the answers, don't know what to do, and aren't willing to put in the work. They figure, "Why not just rob the next guy?" There is also the issue of "I like the way their eggs appear to look, so I'll order them that way. They look tasty, even though I haven't tasted them yet." You have to know how you like your own eggs, even if you figure that out by ordering them the way others do first and tweaking them so they're just right for you.

CHAPTER 14

The Final Frontier: Be Willing to Eat Your Own Dog Food

When you're the only voice left in the room, are you listening?

Being honest in terms of what was a priority and what wasn't was a big growth point for me as it tied back to feeling as though I failed at something or had a fear of an area in which I might fail. What I learned is that sometimes we have to be honest about the bandwidth we have available to us. In order to complete our life tasks, we sometimes have to prioritize and knock them out one at a time.

I refer to this as "eating your own dog food." You have to be able to eat your own words when it comes to the priorities in your life. Doing so really creates perspective in terms of what is most important, because none of us can do it all; at least, not all at once. And realizing we can't do it all at once is often the best-tasting dog-food moment of one's awareness journey!

I'm aware that when my stress is up, I go to a certain place. I'm not as patiently aware, so things get more personal, I get agitated, etc. What's being triggered in these moments is that I'm burning the candle at both ends at a very fast rate and know that I may not be running as efficiently as I could be. I don't have the luxury of planning; I have to just do it. It's therefore going to be sloppy, in my mind at least, which frustrates me. When it feels like I'm drinking from a firehose and the demand on me is super high, my fuse becomes shorter.

We all have advice to give or at times a solution to someone else's problem. We are often quick to offer up that solution, and in many cases, while it may be sound advice, we struggle to incorporate it into our own day-to-day lives. This is why you have to be willing to eat your own dog food. The speed with which you are to offer up a solution to someone else's problems should be mirrored by the speed with which you take that advice for yourself as well.

What I've found is that the more I need to heed a particular piece of advice in my own life, the more likely I am to quickly offer it up to someone else.

When you find yourself wanting to quickly offer up an opinion or piece of advice to someone else, you sometimes have to ask yourself, "Do I do what I am suggesting that they do?" To expand on this, as a parent or leader, we can't hide behind the adage "do as I say not as I do." Trust me, as a parent I step on this landmine all the time. I do it with electronic devices more than anything. Recognizing that I encourage my daughters not to be so dependent on their own electronic devices and having a rule at the dinner table that there are no devices allowed was a moment for me. I couldn't tell my girls to get off their devices and be present and not do the same! I had to call BS on myself and be honest about whether or not there really was likely to be a life-altering message or notification coming through on my device that needed to keep me from being present during face-to-face time with family and friends.

The wake-up call that it was time for me to eat my own dog food came when it was clear based on my actions that the device had more priority than my family had. It's hard to say I'm all about my family when my device gets more time with me then they do! A lot of people talk. The question is, would you eat what's coming out of your own mouth? If not, maybe you need to go back and rethink your play.

CHAPTER 15

See Yourself Through Others' Eyes

I want to end on one simple yet complex point: it's time for you to see the real you! Even the journey of writing this book has opened my eyes to seeing myself more clearly. Before I began writing, when I was hesitantly swaying between I think I want to... and What am I getting myself into?, Kelley said to me, "I want you to write this book so that you can finally see yourself through my eyes."

After she said that, and upon thinking about what others say and have said about me—things I often deflect as untrue because I'm trying to exist in a space of humility—it's a really important perspective to have. No matter who we are, we look in the mirror and see a "normal" person. Others look at us and see people who can accomplish anything we put our minds to. We are typically not good at celebrating how far we've already come. We will continue to create new goals. We will continue to have to know our why. We will continue to have to know our what. And, through it all, I promise that you're far more than you tell yourself that you are most of the time.

The statement that Kelley made stuck with me through the writing, and it's helped to frame this last chapter. I think that, in the past, I ran from thoughts of my own value and impact. This didn't come from a lack of confidence nor is it intended as any sort of Debbie Downer statement. It came from a place of operating in what I've come to believe is normal day-to-day life. I don't come from a rocky childhood, and I haven't had a particularly challenging life (at least, compared to several of my friends and co-workers), so I have felt for some time that I'm "just a lucky guy" who doesn't have much of a story to tell. In reality, we all have a story; we just have to take a minute to see ourselves the way others see us.

So, while this is the final chapter of the book, it begins a new chapter in my journey of self-awareness. This new chapter for me is titled Legacy, and it's all about seeing what my actions have built and how I have impacted my family by being self-aware and having a thirst to be the best version of myself each and every day.

When I committed to making some changes in my own life with regard to self-awareness, I realized that I had two points of misconception—one going into the time period of change and another during the process. Going into the change, my misconception was, "It can't be done." Human nature causes us to place self-doubt, and it's not until we push through the commitment to change that we become aware of all our untapped potential.

Even today, I struggle at the entry point to change and continue to be intrigued as to why we all struggle with it, no matter our level of success. In You Can't Hurt Me, David Goggins speaks on how to build mental toughness and overcome the fact that the mind wants to protect you from the pain or exertion that any activity will cause. While Goggins' chosen adventures often border on the extreme, there is truth in the notion that it's human nature to quit or exit from anything we perceive to be difficult. The unknown will always be difficult, given that we commonly fear what we don't know. Or, is it that we simply don't place it as a priority in life at that moment?

I believe that the two concepts blend together as our minds place value on any particular change. We analyze, to some degree, the mental, emotional, and physical impact it's going to require to complete the task and immediately start having doubts.

I know that many can relate to the pain that the change process of changing one's diet often brings. Talk about doubt—in those instances you tend to have it to some degree all the way through the process!

That's why those who have had success changing their diets or exercise habits employ a key phrase that makes complete sense: "It's a lifestyle change!" It's not a fad or a phase they are attempting. They are 100 percent committed to complete change, and that kind of commitment doesn't come easily. It involves a long transition process with many stumbling blocks along the way.

We have to challenge our thoughts more, because the mere thought that we're going to do things differently isn't the right one with which to walk into change. Instead, we should challenge that statement by asking, "Am I doing things the way I was intended to do them?" After all, how will we ever truly know if we aren't willing to first break what we think works?

It is my hope that you truly see the real you, and that you live a life of self-awareness, intent, and action. The truth? I feel like I'm just getting started at this point. I go to bed every night—even after a hard day—thinking with a chuckle, "The best is yet to come." I know this to be true because I've unlocked myself. I've gotten out of my own way. And everything I do is both consciously and subconsciously driven by my self-awareness.

ACKNOWLEDGEMENTS

To my wife, Kelley—your unconditional love and support for me has never wavered through the years. You believe in me more than I think at times I believe in myself, and no amount of words could ever express how lucky I am to do life with you! Dare I say "Yo Adrien I did it" LOL Rocky Humor.

To my daughters, Sydney, Samantha, and Sofia—you are and will always be my greatest accomplishment in life. Know that you are always capable of more and chase your dreams! But every minute of every day just know Daddy will always love you Moore!

To my family—I wouldn't be here without you. Thank you to my dad for instilling the values and principles that have shaped me into the person I am today. To my stepdad, who has passed, your mentorship and love will never be forgotten.

To my mother-in-law and father-in-law—I don't know if I can put into words how much I love and appreciate you both. Your love and support for all my craziness through the years means the world to me.

To my brother and sister—while we are all over the country/world, know that I am always in your corner and love you.

To my brother-in-law—your unconditional support and friendship are invaluable to me. Your potential is limitless.

Friends and mentors—your love and support mean so much to me. I hope I have given as much to you as you have given to me. Many of you played a role in making this book possible. Thank you again for listening, pushing back, being direct, and sometimes just calling me out.

Lastly, to my Mom—thank you for bringing two amazing men into my life, and most importantly, for showing me how to adapt to change and overcome life challenges.

ABOUT THE AUTHOR

Dan Moore is a big-idea thinker and strategist currently serving as president of a software company. A devoted husband and father of three, he lives with his family in Scottsdale, Arizona. Despite his commitment to self-awareness (or perhaps because of it), he remains steadfast in his dislike of tomatoes.

Facebook.com/DanMoore.1022

Instagram.com/MooreOfDan

twitter.com/mooreofdan

www.linkedin.com/in/MooreOfDan/

www.DoMooreGetMore.com